Elkhonon Goldberg, Ph.D., ABPP/ABCN (consultant) is a clinical professor of neurology at New York University School of Medicine, a diplomate of the American Board of Professional Psychology/American Board of Clinical Neuropsychology, and director of The East-West Science and Education Foundation. Dr. Goldberg created the Manhattan-based Cognitive Enhancement Program, a fitness center for the brain, and is author of the international best-selling books *The Wisdom Paradox: How Your Mind Can Grow as Your Brain Grows Older* and *The Executive Brain: Frontal Lobes and the Civilized Mind.*

Julie K. Cohen is a puzzle developer, puzzle consultant, author, and freelance writer. She has published numerous math puzzle books, and her puzzles for children and adults appear in national magazines, Web sites, puzzle books, cellular phone games, and DVDs. To learn more about Cohen, visit her Web site, http://www.JulieKCohen.com.

Amy Reynaldo, the author of *How to Conquer the New York Times Crossword Puzzle,* created the first crossword blog (Diary of a Crossword Fiend) and reviews 1,500 crosswords a year. She is a top-10 finisher at the American Crossword Puzzle Tournament.

Puzzle Constructors: Michael Adams, Cihan Altay, Myles Callum, Philip Carter, Kelly Clark, Barry Clarke, Conceptis Puzzles, Don Cook, Jeanette Dall, Mark Danna, Josie Faulkner, Adrian Fisher, Ray Hamel, Luke Haward, Marilynn Huret, Lloyd King, Dan Meinking, Kate Mepham, David Millar, Dan Moore, Michael Moreci, Elsa Neal, Alan Olschwang, Dave Roberts, Marylin Roberts, Stephen Ryder, Gianni Sarcone, Pete Sarjeant, Paul Seaburn, Fraser Simpson, Terry Stickels, Howard Tomlinson

Illustrators: Hyelim An, Elizabeth Gerber, Nicole H. Lee, Jay Sato, Shavan R. Spears, Jen Torche

ISBN-13: 978-1-60553-343-8
ISBN-10: 1-60553-343-2

Manufactured in China.

8 7 6 5 4 3 2 1

Puzzles to Flex You
Mental Muscle

Consultant: Elkhonon Goldberg, Ph.D.

Publications International, Ltd.

Contents

A Cognitive Workout

The fountain of youth exists only in folklore and fairy tales, but that hasn't stopped professionals, laypeople, and everyone in between from attempting to uncover the secrets behind good health and longevity. We all want to stay young and active in order to lead fulfilling lives, but to achieve this, we have to keep our bodies *and* our minds in top shape. How do we do this? Well, there is plenty of information regarding the care of our bodies, but relatively little attention has been paid to the importance of taking care of our minds. That's why this publication is so valuable. *Brain Games™: Puzzles to Flex Your Mental Muscle* is an excellent resource that will help you keep your brain fit for life.

The human brain thrives on learning and experiencing new things—it is stimulated by both novelty and challenge. If something is routine or too easy, our brains are essentially operating on autopilot—which doesn't require a lot of mental attention and does little to boost cerebral strength. By exposing ourselves to new activities and information, we are exercising our brains in a way that will keep them sharp and focused.

To maintain cognitive fitness, you have to get your head in the game (pun intended). "Use it or lose it!" should be your motto from now on, and working the puzzles in this publication is a great way to put those words into action so you can start to benefit from them.

Researchers use the term "cognitive reserve" to explain the importance of building brain power from an early age. In doing so, you are creating a "cushion" that will keep your brain in good

operating order as you get older. But it's never too late to start working on brain fitness. "Now" is the best time to learn to play a musical instrument, to enroll in a new class—and to take advantage of all this publication has to offer.

Take a few minutes to familiarize yourself with the wide variety of puzzles in this book (as well as their levels of difficulty). Different kinds of puzzles stimulate different parts of the brain, and you should exercise as many of those areas as possible. To help you choose the puzzles that will provide the most benefit, we've labeled each one with the cognitive functions it exercises (computation, language, logic, and memory are just a few). Consider doing a variety of puzzles each day so that you don't limit the scope of your workout. Like physical fitness, cognitive fitness can be the result of consistently challenging—and varied— workouts.

Finally, don't forget that puzzles are a lot of fun to solve—think of the simple enjoyment you derive from working a crossword or finding your way through a twisting maze. The pleasure of sitting back and doing a puzzle is not only relaxing—it can also help relieve stress after a long day. Another

great thing about this publication is that it's small enough to carry anywhere: to the park, the doctor's office, or on a trip out of town. Whenever you have a chance, turn your downtime into brain-boosting time—and think of the fun you'll have while doing it!

ANALYSIS

Name Calling

Decipher the encoded words in the quip below using the numbers and letters on the phone pad. Remember that each number can stand for 3 or 4 possible letters.

A 9–4–6–5–3 fool is half a 7–7–6–7–4–3–8.

(handwritten above: w h o l e ... p r o p h e t)

Quic-Kross

LANGUAGE

This is a crossword puzzle with a twist. Use the clues to solve the puzzle. When complete, the circled letters will spell out a "mystery word."

Across

1. To place

2. Negative

3. Floor cover

Down

4. Perform

5. Eat (past tense)

6. What person?

Mystery word clue: Edible tuber

GENERAL KNOWLEDGE

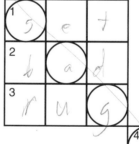

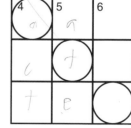

Answers on page 165.

You Are Here

…and the taxi meter is ticking. This professional building is a maze of corridors and cubicles. Elevators are available, but there are no stairs. And over-stressed office workers won't give you directions to the exit. Why, oh why, did you ever come in here? Doesn't matter now—time to get moving!

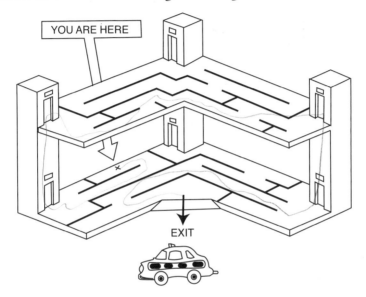

A Puzzling Perspective

Mentally arrange the lettered balls from large to small in the correct order to spell an 11-letter word.

Clue: For the time being

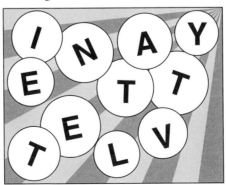

Answers on page 165. **7**

Star Power

Fill in each empty square in the grid so that each star is surrounded by the numbers 1 through 8 with no repeats.

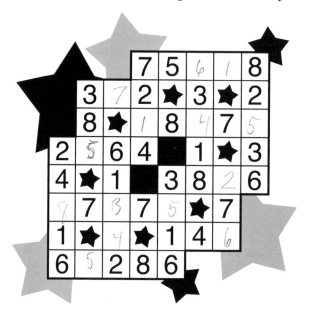

Spell Math!

Spell out numbers in the blanks below to obtain the correct solution. Numbers are used only once and range from 1 to 20. A letter has been given to get you started.

$$\underline{O} \ N \ \underline{E} \ +$$

$$\underline{S \ i \ x \ t \ e \ e \ n} \ =$$

$$\underline{S \ e \ v \ e \ n \ t \ e \ e \ n}$$

Answers on page 165.

PLANNING LOGIC

COMPUTATION ANALYSIS

Word Jigsaw

Fit the pieces into the frame to form common, uncapitalized words reading across and down. There's no need to rotate the pieces; they'll fit as shown, with each piece used exactly once.

LANGUAGE PLANNING

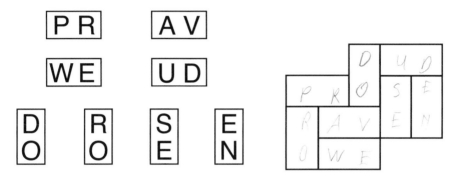

Trivia on the Brain

A study from 2003 found that 18 percent of people surveyed never or rarely dreamed in color, but in 1942 as many as 71 percent never or rarely had. It's amazing the difference TV and movies have made!

Perfect Score

Make 3 successful hits so that the sum of the numbers is 100. Double and triple scores do not apply. Numbers may be used more than once.

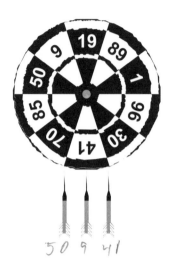

50 9 41

1-2-3

Place the numbers 1, 2, or 3 in the circles below. The challenge is to have only these 3 numbers in each connected row and column—no number should repeat. Any combination is allowed.

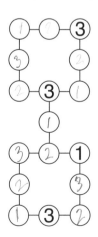

Answers on page 165.

Natural Disasters

The grid contains terms associated with natural disasters. The words can be found in a straight line horizontally, vertically, or diagonally. They may be read either backward or forward. The leftover letters spell out a fact about natural disasters.

AVALANCHE   ERUPTION   LANDSLIDE

BLIZZARD   FAMINE   MUD FLOW

CYCLONE   FLOOD   PLAGUE

DROUGHT   HAILSTORM   SANDSTORM

EARTHQUAKE   HEAT WAVE

EPIDEMIC   LAHAR

```
I  N  E  H  C  N  A  L  A  V  A  T  H  E
L  A  S  T  D  E  O  C  A  D  E  T  H  E
A  V  E  P  R  R  B  L  I  Z  Z  A  R  D  A
M  U  D  F  L  O  W  G  T  R  E  A  N  N
M  E  E  U  A  A  L  D  E  P  A  A  T  H
T  R  N  O  L  L  G  F  R  O  U  H  M  D
I  S  O  I  E  K  A  U  Q  H  T  R  A  E
A  S  L  T  M  C  I  M  E  D  I  P  E  L
T  E  C  R  S  A  N  D  S  T  O  R  M  S
W  A  Y  S  A  L  F  T  H  G  U  O  R  D
B  O  C  U  E  D  I  L  S  D  N  A  L  T
S  I  X  T  Y  S  E  A  V  E  N  T  H  F
O  E  V  A  W  T  A  E  H  U  S  A  N  D
```

Leftover letters: _IN THE LAST DECADE_
the Average Death toll from Disasters
was ABOUt Sixty Seventhousand

XOXO

Place an X or an O inside each empty cell of the grid so that there appears no row, column, or diagonal with 4 consecutive cells with the same letter.

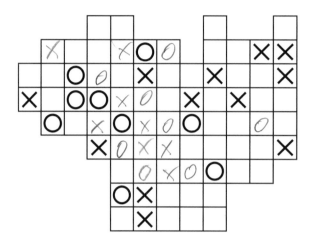

Word Ladder

Use the clues to change just one letter on each line to go from the top word to the bottom word. Do not change the order of the letters. You must have a common English word at each step.

TWO

_T O O_   in addition

_T O N_   heavy weight

_I O N_   charged particle

_I N N_   place to stay the night

_I N K_   pen filler

_I R K_   vex

ARK

Answers on page 165.

NASCAR Weekend
by Alpha Sleuth™

Move each of the letters below into the grid to form common words. You will use each letter once. The letters in the numbered cells of the grid correspond to the letters in the phrase at the bottom. Completing the grid will help you complete the phrase and vice versa. When finished, the grid and phrase should be filled with valid words, and you will have used all the letters in the letter set.

Hint: The numbered cells in the grid are arranged alphabetically, so the letter in the cell marked 1 will appear in the alphabet before the letter in the cell marked 2, and so on.

Sudoku

Use deductive logic to complete the grid so that each row, each column, and each 3 by 3 box contains the numbers 1 through 9 in some order. The solution is unique.

5	2	6	7	4	1	9	8	3
8	1	7	2	9	3	5	6	4
3	4	9	6	5	8	2	1	7
6	9	1	3	8	5	4	7	2
2	8	4	9	1	7	3	5	6
7	5	3	4	2	6	1	9	8
4	3	8	5	7	9	6	2	1
1	6	5	8	3	2	7	4	9
9	7	2	1	6	4	8	3	5

Hashi

Each circle represents an island, with the number inside indicating the number of bridges connected to it. Draw bridges between islands using the number given, but there can be no more than 2 bridges going in the same direction and there must be a continuous path connecting all islands. Bridges can only be vertical or horizontal and may not cross islands or other bridges. We've drawn some bridges to get you started.

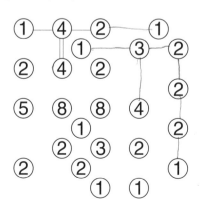

Answers on page 166.

Elevator Words

Like an elevator, words move up and down the "floors" of this puzzle. Starting with the first answer, the second word from each answer carries down to become the first word of the following answer. With the clues given, complete the puzzle.

1. Car _pool_

2. _pool_ _party_

3. _party_ _line_

4. _line_ _dance_

5. _dance_ _floor_

6. _floor_ _board_

7. _board_ Game

Clues

1. It may travel in a special lane

2. Some summertime fun

3. Pols often follow it

4. The Electric Slide, for example

5. Ballroom feature

6. Something to step on

7. Monopoly, e.g

Alley Shots

Across

1. Mercedes-_____
5. Confident of one's correctness
9. Former United rival
12. Tortoise-hare meeting
13. Spanish bull
14. Shred
15. Disney's Aladdin, e.g.
16. Defeatist statement
18. Nickels and dimes
20. Boat measured in cubits
21. First known binary star
24. Point, as a gun
27. Muslim religious title
30. Therefore
31. Find fortune, perhaps
34. Aquatic bird with a forked tail
35. Musical symbol
36. Your, in Paris
37. Gas station name
39. License plate
41. Street urchin
47. Surpass
49. Doing fine
50. Ingot
51. They've split up
52. Trivial
53. Current office holders
54. Purges
55. "Good _____" (Food Network series)

Down

1. They were burned for women's lib
2. Old West law officer Wyatt
3. Campus sports org.
4. Striped mammal
5. Simple drawings of people
6. Clothes closet menace
7. _____ Major (Big Dipper)
8. "_____ Fly Now" ("Rocky" theme)
9. Oscar-winning movie for John Wayne
10. Used to be
11. Grow old
17. Stared at
19. "CHiPs" star Estrada
22. Unfriendly person
23. A ton
24. Movie terrier
25. Short piece of news
26. He had a neighborhood on TV
28. Major address?
29. It rests on box springs
32. Acquire
33. Votes in the affirmative
38. River mammal

40. Garden statue
42. Move down the runway
43. Supplemented, with "out"
44. Furniture store chain
45. Scalp line
46. Vision organs
47. Kimono sash
48. Mover's vehicle

Cross Count

All the letters of the alphabet have been assigned a value from 1 through 9, as demonstrated in the box below. Fill in the grid with common English words so that the rows and columns add up correctly.

1	2	3	4	5	6	7	8	9
A	B	C	D	E	F	G	H	I
J	K	L	M	N	O	P	Q	R
S	T	U	V	W	X	Y	Z	

t	h	A	t	13
e	a	s	e	12
A	r	k	s	13
l	e	s	t	11
11	23	5	10	

Trivia on the Brain

On average, the male brain is slightly bigger than the female brain—but the differences in weight or size don't mean there are differences in mental ability.

Answer on page 166.

Cluster

Fill in each grape so the number in descending rows is the total of the neighboring numbers from the row above it. Each grape contains a positive whole number. Numbers can be repeated.

Calcu-doku

Use arithmetic and deductive logic to complete the grid so that each row and each column contains the numbers 1 through 4 in some order. Numbers in each outlined set of squares combine to produce the number in the top corner using the mathematical sign indicated.

5+ 3	5+ 4	1	2 2
2	3 3	8× 4	4+ 1
4× 4	1	2	3
2/ 1	2	7+ 3	4

Honeycomb Maze

Can you find your way through this maze?

START

END

Spell Math!

Spell out numbers in the blanks below to obtain the correct solution. Numbers are used only once and range from 1 to 20. A letter has been given to get you started.

$$\underline{\text{t w o}}^{+}$$
$$\text{E}\underline{\text{l e v e n}}^{=}$$
$$\underline{\text{t h i r t e e n}}$$

Answers on pages 166–167.

Crazy Circles

Only 2 of these circles are the same. Look carefully to find them. Draw a line connecting the 2 circles.

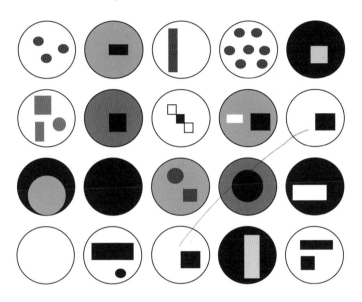

ATTENTION · VISUAL SEARCH

Word Ladder

Use the clues to change just one letter on each line to go from the top word to the bottom word. Do not change the order of the letters. You must have a common English word at each step.

CRAVE

CRANE   vast metal lifting structure

CRAZE   it's sweeping the nation

GRAZE   mild wound

GRACE   amazing

TRACE

LANGUAGE · PLANNING

Word-a-Maze: Vital Sign

Travel in sequence through the puzzle from the left side to the right, using each numbered clue to determine the correct word. Connect adjacent words together with a common letter to proceed through the maze. Some letters are already given. The first and last words tie into the title.

1. Vampire snack

2. Dent

3. Glimmer

4. First president

5. From dusk on

6. Relate

7. Joke response

8. Place to eat

9. To drive down

10. Like 2 peas in
a ____

11. Cloudy, wet,
and cold

12. 365 days

13. Allotment

14. Most loud

15. Canvas cover

16. Support

17. Urge

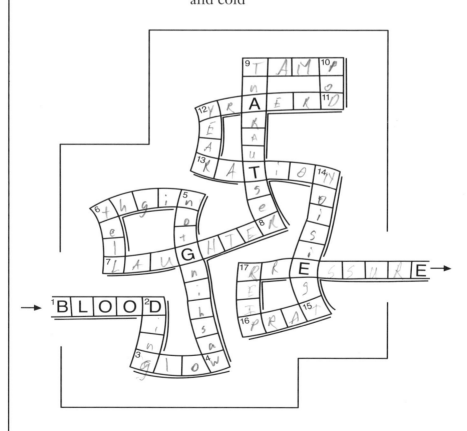

Answers on page 167.

Kakuro

Place a number from 1 through 9 in each empty cell so that the sum of each vertical or horizontal run (rows and columns extending from already numbered cells) equals the number at the top or on the left of that run. Numbers may not be repeated in any run, and runs end at dark-colored squares.

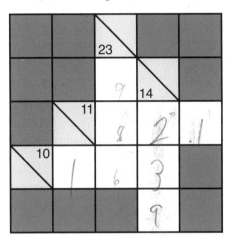

L'adder

Starting at the bottom rung, use the numbers 1 through 9 to add up to the top number. Numbers can only be used once. There's a catch though: The precise sums must be met along the way.

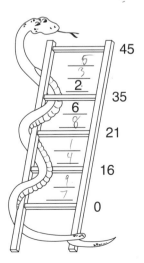

Answers on page 167. **23**

Active Scramblegram

Four 8-letter words, all of which revolve around the same theme, have been jumbled. Unscramble each word and write the answer in the accompanying space. Next, transfer the letters in the shaded boxes into the keyword space and unscramble the 9-letter word that goes with the theme. The theme for this puzzle is games and sports.

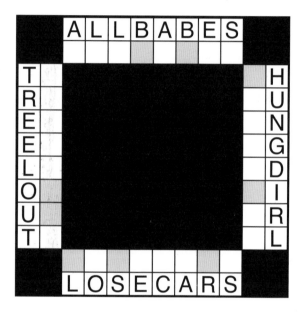

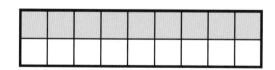

Answers on page 167.

Add-a-Letter

Fill in each set of blanks below. Answer the first clue in each with a 3-letter word. Add a letter to the beginning of the first word to answer the second clue. Then add a letter to the end of the second word to answer the third clue.

1. a) What you hear with — *ear*
   b) Endure — *bear*
   c) Chin hair — *beard*

2. a) Male sheep — *ram*
   b) Pack tightly — *cram*
   c) Painful spasm — *cramp*

3. a) Hole or hollow — *pit*
   b) _____ and polish — *spit*
   c) Malice — *spite*

4. a) Painting, sculpture, etc. — *art*
   b) Section — *part*
   c) Birthday celebration — *party*

5. a) Chop off — *lop*
   b) Slush — *slop*
   c) Hill — *slope*

6. a) Monkey — *ape*
   b) Cloak — *cape*
   c) Frolic — *caper*

7. a) Male people — *Men*
   b) Final word in prayer — *amen*
   c) Alter — *amend*

Arrow Web

Shade in some of the arrows so that each arrow in the grid points to exactly 1 shaded arrow.

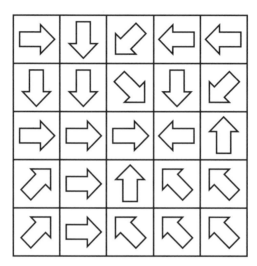

Sudoku

Use deductive logic to complete the grid so that each row, each column, and each 3 by 3 box contains the numbers 1 through 9 in some order. The solution is unique.

6	8	1	5	2	3	7	4	9
9	2	5	8	7	4	6	1	3
3	7	4	9	6	1	2	5	8
5	9	8	3	1	6	4	7	2
7	6	3	2	4	5	8	9	1
1	4	2	7	9	8	5	3	6
4	1	7	6	8	9	3	2	5
8	3	9	4	5	2	1	6	7
2	5	6	1	3	7	9	8	4

Answers on page 168.

Marbles

Place 9 marbles into the grid without having any touch one another, not even diagonally. There are some walls, represented by thick lines, that block the view of the marbles. Marbles must not "see" each other in a horizontal or vertical direction. We've placed 1 to get you started.

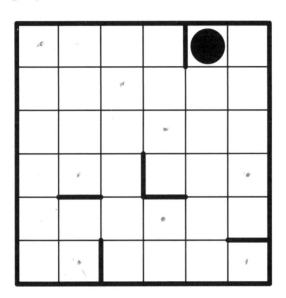

 Trivia on the Brain

It's a myth that alcohol destroys brain cells. But it is true that alcohol weakens connections between neurons and makes new cells grow less quickly, which interferes with brain activity and causes serious damage.

VISUAL SEARCH

ATTENTION

Weather Word Search

Every word listed below is contained within this group of letters. Words can be found horizontally, vertically, or diagonally. They may read either backward or forward.

CLOUD
COLD
FAIR
FOG
FROST
HOT
HUMID
ICE
LIGHTNING
RAIN
SLEET
SNOW
STORM
SUNSHINE
TORNADO
WIND

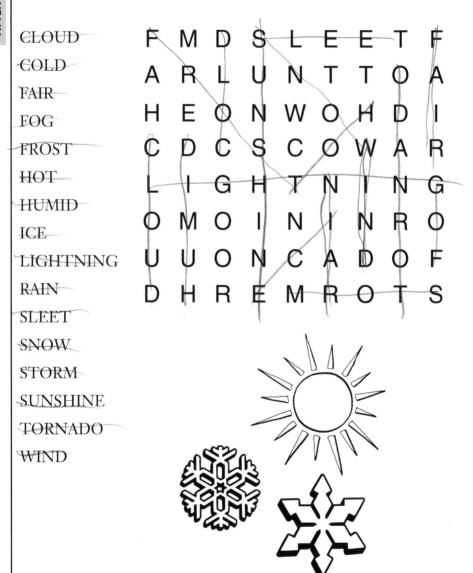

F M D S L E E T F
A R L U N T T O A
H E O N W O H D I
C D C S C O W A R
L I G H T N I N G
O M O I N I N R O
U U O N C A D O F
D H R E M R O T S

28

Answers on page 168.

1-2-3

Place the numbers 1, 2, or 3 in the circles below. The challenge is to have only these 3 numbers in each connected row and column—no number should repeat. Any combination is allowed.

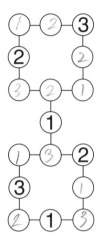

XOXO

Place an X or an O inside each empty cell of the grid so that there appears no row, column, or diagonal with 4 consecutive cells with the same letter.

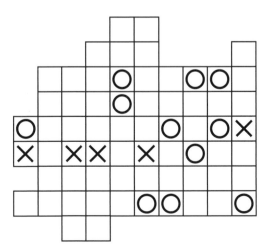

PLANNING

LANGUAGE

Word Jigsaw

Fit the pieces into the frame to form common, uncapitalized words reading across and down. There's no need to rotate the pieces; they'll fit as shown, with each piece used exactly once.

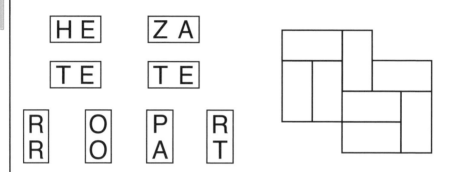

VISUAL LOGIC

COMPUTATION

Perfect Score

Make 3 successful hits so that the sum of the numbers is 100. Double and triple scores do not apply. Numbers may be used more than once.

Answers on page 168.

Clone It!

Use the grid dots as a guide to split the shaded shape into 2 smaller shapes that are either identical or mirror one another.

For a hint, study the example illustrations at the bottom.

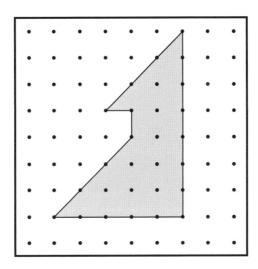

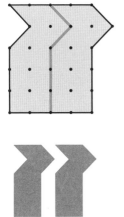

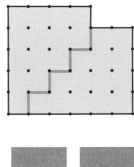

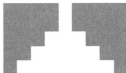

This Is the Day

Across

1. "Bam!"
4. 'Vette roof option
8. Self-satisfied
12. Lyric poem
13. Roll call response
14. Chopped liver spread
15. Sunrise devotion
18. Primps
19. Revolted
20. Mai _____ (cocktail)
21. Monthly rent outlay, e.g.: abbr.
22. Vehicle for school kids
25. Charged particle
27. Vaulted church recess
31. Siestas
35. Bean source of tofu
36. Medical care grp.
37. Feline pet
38. Sought elected office
41. Residential suffix
43. Draw, as football game
46. Powerful Greek deities
50. Factory guard, after closing time
52. Swiss painter Paul
53. Confederate General Robert _____
54. One _____ time
55. Witnessed
56. Actor Alan of "Shane"
57. Emulate a bunny

Down

1. Ceremonial splendor
2. Smell
3. "The Way We _____"
4. Where things seem to disappear into
5. Stress
6. Assn.
7. Enliven
8. Michigan State athlete
9. BLT spread
10. Sport _____ (family cars)
11. Actor Richard of "Pretty Woman"
16. Butterfly catcher's tool
17. Tach reading: abbr.
22. _____-relief (sculptural style)
23. ET's ride
24. Pig's digs
26. Japanese drama
28. Lobbyist employer, for short
29. Health club feature
30. Winter hrs. in Boston
32. Like pottery
33. Left out
34. Observed
39. Little island, in Britain
40. Staircase support
42. Archaic verb ending
43. Fountain pen fluids
44. Egypt's river

45. "The African Queen" screenwriter James
47. Asian nursemaid
48. Defense grp. since 1949
49. Click of the fingers
51. Apple pie _____ mode

1 P	2 O	3 W		4 T	5 T	6 O	7 P		8 S	9 M	10 U	11 G
12 O	d	e		13 h	e	r	e		14 P	A	T	E
15 m	o	r	16 n	i	n	G	P	17 R	a	Y	e	R
18 P	r	e	e	n	s		19 U	P	r	o	S	e
		20 T	a	i		21 a	m	t				
22 R	23 u	24 S		25 I	o	26 N			27 a	28 P	29 S	30 e
31	f	32 e	R	n		33	34 n					
35 S	o	y	a		36 h	m	o		37 C	a	t	
		38 R	39 a	40 n		41 A	V	42 e				
43 I	44 N	45		I		46	t		47 A	48 N	49 S	
50 n	i	g	h	t	w	51 a	t	c	h	m	A	n
52 k	l			53 F	L	e	e		54 a	t	a	
55 S	e	e	n	56 a					57 h	o	p	

Kakuro

Place a number from 1 through 9 in each empty cell so that the sum of each vertical or horizontal run (rows and columns extending from already numbered cells) equals the number at the top or on the left of that run. Numbers may not be repeated in any run, and runs end at dark-colored squares.

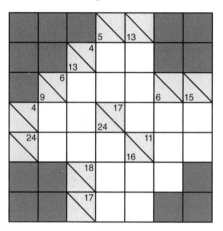

Cross Count

All the letters of the alphabet have been assigned a value from 1 through 9, as demonstrated in the box below. Fill in the grid with common English words so that the rows and columns add up correctly.

1	2	3	4	5	6	7	8	9
A	B	C	D	E	F	G	H	I
J	K	L	M	N	O	P	Q	R
S	T	U	V	W	X	Y	Z	

	8	7	17
W			16
	7	2	15
13	21	14	

Answers on page 169.

Perfect Harmony
by Alpha Sleuth™

Move each of the letters below into the grid to form common words. You will use each letter once. The letters in the numbered cells of the grid correspond to the letters in the phrase at the bottom. Completing the grid will help you complete the phrase and vice versa. When finished, the grid and phrase should be filled with valid words, and you will have used all the letters in the letter set.

Hint: The numbered cells in the grid are arranged alphabetically, so the letter in the cell marked 1 will appear in the alphabet before the letter in the cell marked 2, and so on.

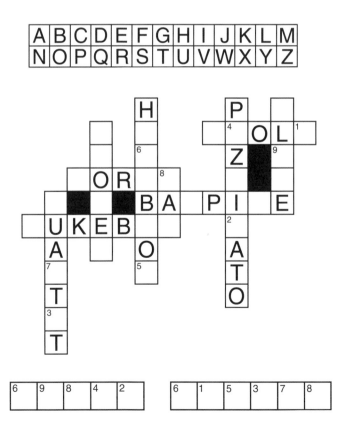

It's a Jungle Out There!

These 8 animals are hidden somewhere in the picture. Can you find and circle them all?

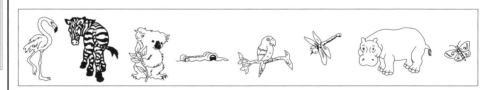

Answer on page 169.

Missing Connections

It's a crossword without the clues! Use the letters below to fill in the empty spaces in the crossword grid. When you are finished, you'll have words that read both across and down, crossword-style.

B E E E E L L N N N O O O O

O P P R R R S T T T T V V W X

Pump Up the Brainpower

Calcu-doku

Use arithmetic and deductive logic to complete the grid so that each row and each column contains the numbers 1 through 5 in some order. Numbers in each outlined set of squares combine to produce the number in the top corner using the mathematical sign indicated.

2/	5	4+		20×
	2/		7+	
15+		2/		2
			11+	
4	5×			

Word Columns

Find the humorous statement by using the letters directly below each of the blank squares. Each letter is used only once. A black square indicates the end of a word.

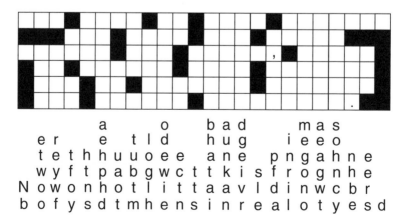

```
            a        o      b a d       m a s
    e r     e    t l d      h u g      i e e o
    t e t h h u u o e e    a n e    p n g a h n e
    w y f t p a b g w c t t k i s f r o g n h e
  N o w o n h o t l i t t a a v l d i n w c b r
  b o f y s d t m h e n s i n r e a l o t y e s d
```

Answers on page 169.

XOXO

Place an X or an O inside each empty cell of the grid so that there appears no row, column, or diagonal with 4 consecutive cells with the same letter.

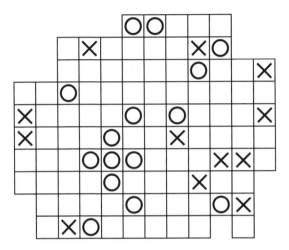

Marbles

Place 8 marbles into the grid without having any touch one another, not even diagonally. There are some walls, represented by thick lines, that block the view of the marbles. Marbles must not "see" each other in a horizontal or vertical direction. We've placed 1 to get you started.

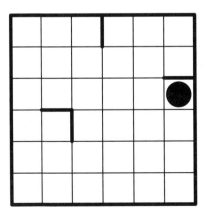

PROBLEM SOLVING

LOGIC

LANGUAGE

COMPUTATION

Cast-a-Word

There are 4 dice, and there are different letters of the alphabet on the 6 faces of each of them (each letter appears only once). Random throws of the dice produced the words in this list. Can you figure out which letters appear on each of the 4 dice?

BOAT	FURY	ROTA
CLAD	JINX	SHOW
CONE	JOIN	SURE
DRAG	MORE	WAVE
FLIT	POEM	ZERO

Cross Count

All the letters of the alphabet have been assigned values from 1 through 9, as demonstrated in the box below. Fill in the grid with common English words so that the rows and columns add up correctly.

1	2	3	4	5	6	7	8	9
A	B	C	D	E	F	G	H	I
J	K	L	M	N	O	P	Q	R
S	T	U	V	W	X	Y	Z	

6	a			20
		6	e	15
		6	2 t	16
2	6	2		15
10	17	23	16	

Answers on page 170.

Pampered Pups

Find the 14 differences between these 2 doggy salon scenes.

Rhyme Time

Each clue leads to a 2-word answer that rhymes, such as BIG PIG or STABLE TABLE. The numbers in parentheses after the clue give the number of letters in each word. For example, "cookware taken from the oven (3, 3)" would be "hot pot."

1. An unusual Christmas gift (4, 4): _____ _____

2. Skip the service (4, 4): _____ _____

3. Where to stay during those days before Easter (4, 4):

_____ _____

4. Blessed netminder (4, 6): _____ _____

5. Best athlete in the congregation (5, 4): _____ _____

6. Least trusted member the church chorus (5, 4):

_____ _____

7. She's in charge of a Church emblem (5, 4):

_____ _____

8. Parishioners' favorite tree (6, 5): _____ _____

9. A poem about an Easter adornment (6, 6):

_____ _____

10. Pester the priest (6, 6): _____ _____

Answers on page 170.

Arrow Web

Shade in some of the arrows so that each arrow in the grid points to exactly 1 shaded arrow.

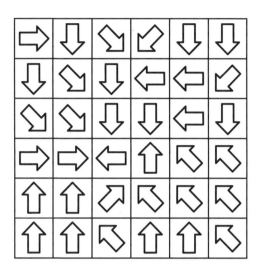

Vex-a-Gon

Place the numbers 1 through 6 into the triangles of each hexagon. The numbers may be in any order, but they do not repeat within each hexagon shape.

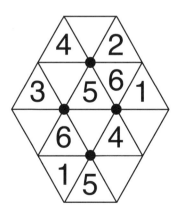

Uncrossed Paths

Draw lines to like symbols (triangle to triangle, star to star) without any line crossing another line.

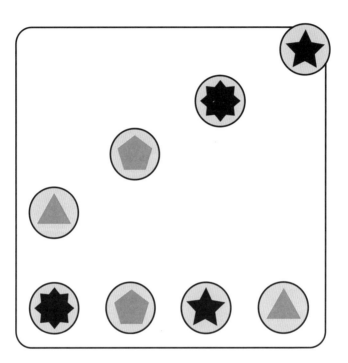

 Trivia on the Brain

Though researchers aren't sure why, studies show test groups that chewed gum had an improved memory of 35 percent when compared with groups that didn't chew. One theory is that insulin, a natural chemical that stimulates the part of the brain related to memory, is released when chewing.

Answer on page 170.

Spelling **B**

Every **B** word listed below is contained within the letter grid. The words can be found in a straight line horizontally, vertically, or diagonally. They can be read either forward or backward. When you have found all the words, the remaining letters will spell a wry observation about this topic.

BAGASSE	BLENNY	BRUSQUERIE
BAILEY	BONSPIEL	BRYOLOGY
BEADLE	BOTRYOIDAL	BULWARKS
BEDIZEN	BOUBOU	BURGONET
BIGHT	BROGAN	BUSTARD

```
B  E  D  I  Z  E  N  M  A  N  Y
B  R  U  S  Q  U  E  R  I  E  E
L  B  O  T  R  Y  O  I  D  A  L
E  R  Y  G  H  A  V  B  E  B  D
N  Y  E  E  A  E  N  S  U  E  A
N  O  T  U  L  N  N  G  S  O  E
Y  L  B  L  E  I  P  S  N  O  B
Y  O  B  U  L  W  A  R  K  S  I
S  G  P  E  L  G  L  B  I  N  G
G  Y  D  R  A  T  S  U  B  B  H
E  E  S  B  U  R  G  O  N  E  T
```

Leftover letters: _____

_____

VISUAL LOGIC
COMPUTATION
LANGUAGE
GENERAL KNOWLEDGE

Perfect Score

Make 3 successful hits so that the sum of the numbers is 100. Double and triple scores do not apply. Numbers may be used more than once.

Elevator Words

Like an elevator, words move up and down the "floors" of this puzzle. Starting with the first answer, the second word from each answer carries down to become the first word of the following answer. With the clues given, complete the puzzle.

Clues

1. Burger side   1. Potato _____

2. Romaine, for one   2. _____ _____

3. Drink garnish   3. _____ _____

4. Relish tray leftover   4. _____ _____

5. Refueling break   5. _____ _____

6. Slam on the brakes   6. _____ _____

7. What the loser drew   7. _____ Straw

Answers on page 171.

Star Power

Fill in each empty square in the grid so that each star is surrounded by the numbers 1 through 8 with no repeats.

Name Calling

Decipher the encoded words in the quip below using the numbers and letters on the phone pad. Remember that each number can stand for 3 or 4 possible letters.

A mother 8–6–3–3–7–7–8–2–6–3–7 what a 2–4–4–5–3 does not say.

Revolutionary
Crypto-Quote

Cryptograms are messages in substitution code. Break the code to read the quote and its author. For example, THE SMART CAT might become FVO QWGDF JGF if **F** is substituted for **T, V** for **H, O** for **E,** and so on.

"D KNT BMKR MSBTP TPMGFL

CTOMXTI BLT BVGBL."

—Q.N. KTPNP

A Sequence
Addressing Freedom

Can you complete this sequence?

F S A _____ Y A

Answers on page 171.

You Are Here

...and the taxi meter is ticking. This professional building is a maze of corridors and cubicles. Elevators are local or express only; there are no stairs. And over-stressed office workers won't give you directions to the exit. Why, oh why, did you ever come in here? Doesn't matter now—time to get moving!

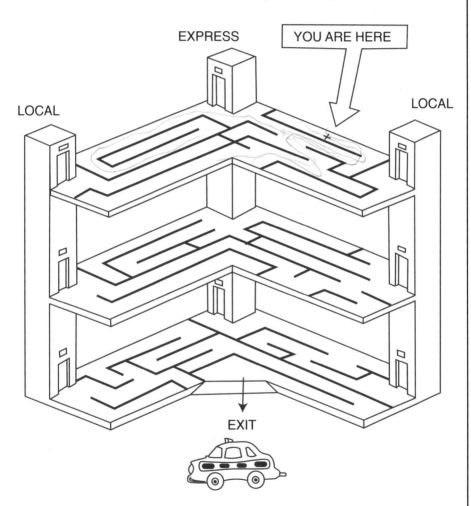

EXPRESS

YOU ARE HERE

LOCAL

LOCAL

EXIT

Daffy Definitions

The 7 entries in this freeform crossword consist of 2-word phrases. But some puzzle imps have worked a little mischief here. They've broken the phrases apart and separated their words. To make matters worse, they've come up with daffy definitions of the phrases. Working with those funny definitions, can you reconstruct the phrases?

Word List:

TALE	VENTURE	JOINT
UP	GLEE	GIVEAWAY
DEAD	TALL	GOD
HAM	CLUB	CURED
SPEED	FED	

The Daffy Definitions:

Across

1. How angry guests leave a banquet?
6. Could it be faster than light?
7. What you get by stretching the truth?

Down

2. Will?
3. Bad actor who's left show biz?
4. Bar hopping?
5. Group of elated optimists?

Answers on page 171.

Cube Count

Imagine that this configuration once was comprised of 64 small cubes (4×4×4). How many cubes are now missing? Assume all rows and columns are complete unless you actually see them end.

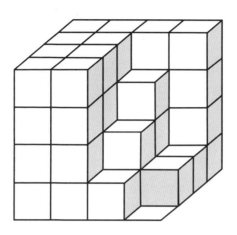

Digital Anagram

What 2 words, formed from different arrangements of the same 7 letters, can be used to complete the sentence below?

I know you like citrus drinks, so I went online and _____

you a coupon for a discount on _____.

Hashi

VISUAL LOGIC

PLANNING

Each circle represents an island, with the number inside indicating the number of bridges connected to it. Draw bridges between islands using the number given, but there can be no more than 2 bridges going in the same direction and there must be a continuous path connecting all islands. Bridges can only be vertical or horizontal and may not cross islands or other bridges. We've drawn some bridges to get you started.

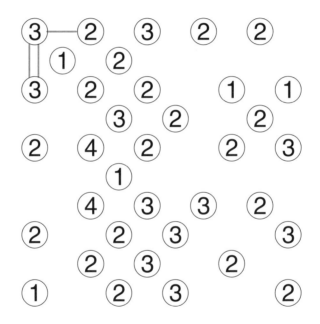

Trivia on the Brain

The word "shrink" comes from "headshrinker," and probably started as a denigrating comparison between psychotherapy and the tribal practice of boiling heads. The first recorded use of the descriptor was in 1966.

Answer on page 172.

Word Ladder

Use the clues to change just one letter on each line to go from the top word to the bottom word. Do not change the order of the letters. You must have a common English word at each step.

SHAVE

SLAVE they do menial work for no pay, but it's immoral

_____ a metamorphic rock which can be cut into thin layers

_____ can be china, or tectonic

PLATO

Sudoku

Use deductive logic to complete the grid so that each row, each column, and each 3 by 3 box contains the numbers 1 through 9 in some order. The solution is unique.

2				6				
	3	1	9		8			
		6	5				8	
	8				4		3	7
7								4
6	1		7				5	
	6				9	5		
			1		5	6	9	
				3				2

ANALYSIS · COMPUTATION

Kakuro

Place a number from 1 through 9 in each empty cell so that the sum of each vertical or horizontal run (rows and columns extending from already numbered cells) equals the number at the top or on the left of that run. Numbers may not be repeated in any run, and runs end at dark-colored squares.

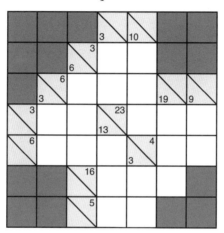

Cluster

Fill in each grape so that the number in descending rows is the total of the neighboring numbers from the row above it. Each grape contains a positive whole number. Numbers can be repeated.

Answers on page 172.

Auto Showcase
by Alpha Sleuth™

Move each of the letters below into the grid to form common words. You will use each letter once. The letters in the numbered cells of the grid correspond to the letters in the phrase at the bottom. Completing the grid will help you complete the phrase and vice versa. When finished, the grid and phrase should be filled with valid words, and you will have used all the letters in the letter set.

Hint: The numbered cells in the grid are arranged alphabetically, so the letter in the cell marked 1 will appear in the alphabet before the letter in the cell marked 2, and so on.

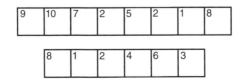

PLANNING

LANGUAGE

Word Jigsaw

Fit the pieces into the frame to form common, uncapitalized words reading across and down. There's no need to rotate the pieces; they'll fit as shown, with each piece used exactly once.

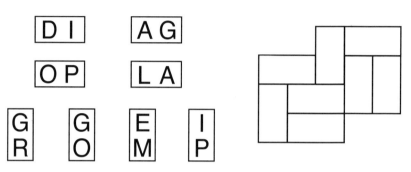

COMPUTATION

ANALYSIS

Spell Math!

Spell out numbers in the blanks below to obtain the correct solution. Numbers are used only once and range from 1 to 20. A letter has been given to get you started.

+

—— —— —— —— ——

T __ __ __ __ __

=

—— —— —— —— —— —— ——

Answers on page 172.

Elevator Words

Like an elevator, words move up and down the "floors" of this puzzle. Starting with the first answer, the second word from each answer carries down to become the first word of the following answer. With the clues given, complete the puzzle.

1. Live _____

2. _____ _____

3. _____ _____

4. _____ _____

5. _____ _____

6. _____ _____

7. _____ Lift

Clues

1. Very active and energetic person

2. Charcoal grill accessory

3. Drought danger

4. Call to leave a building

5. Sleep interrupter

6. This could be analog or digital

7. Sort of cosmetic surgery

Presidential Scramblegram

Four 8-letter words, all of which revolve around the same theme, have been jumbled. Unscramble the words and write the answers in the accompanying space. Next, transfer the letters that are in the shaded boxes into the shaded keyword space and unscramble the 9-letter word that goes with the theme. The theme for this puzzle is presidents.

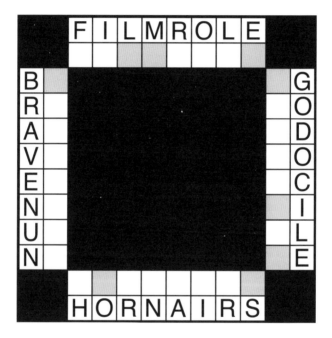

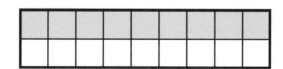

Answers on page 173.

Vex-a-Gon

Place the numbers 1 through 6 into the triangles of each hexagon. The numbers may be in any order, but they do not repeat within each hexagon shape.

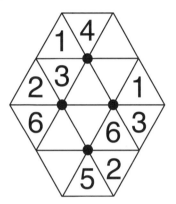

Cross Count

All the letters of the alphabet have been assigned values from 1 through 9, as demonstrated in the box below. Fill in the grid with common English words so that the rows and columns add up correctly. The completed grid will contain the beginning of a magical phrase and a Hardy heroine.

1	2	3	4	5	6	7	8	9
A	B	C	D	E	F	G	H	I
J	K	L	M	N	O	P	Q	R
S	T	U	V	W	X	Y	Z	

2	1	7	5	
				15
	b	r		13
	³l	⁶o		14
				9
8	11	23	9	

Dissection

Separate the figure into 2 identical parts following the grid lines. The parts may be rotated and/or mirrored.

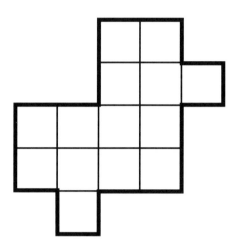

Trivia on the Brain

Did you know you're a musical composer? It's true—the Department of Homeland Security is currently working with scientists to read a person's brain waves and "translate" them into musical notes. The recording is then converted into two unique musical compositions designed to improve productivity or relaxation for the said person. Right now they're testing it out on a select group of firefighters. But they hope to use this method to aid all emergency responders someday by sharpening their reflexes during a crisis and calming their nerves afterward.

Answer on page 173.

L'adder

Starting at the bottom rung, use the numbers 1 through 9 to add up to the top number. Numbers can only be used once. There's a catch though: The precise sums must be met along the way.

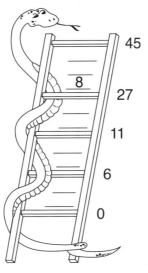

45

8

27

11

6

0

Calcu-doku

Use arithmetic and deductive logic to complete the grid so that each row and each column contains the numbers 1 through 4 in some order. Numbers in each outlined set of squares combine to produce the number in the top corner using the mathematical sign indicated.

8×		4+	
3+		3-	1-
12×	2-		
		6+	

Prince Albert

Across

1. Gas bill info
6. Pirate ship board
11. Lawmaker of old Athens
12. Pujols was National League _____ of the Year in 2001
13. "And best _____, it's free!"
14. With 44-Across, Pujols has the highest career _____ among active players
15. Team that Pujols plays for
17. RBI and ERA, e.g.
18. Navy commando
19. Give fizz to
23. Louts
29. See 4-Down
30. Pujols's home stadium in St. Louis
31. Plants firmly
33. Manage a museum
34. Light bulb unit
36. June honoree
39. Defensive position at which Pujols excels
44. See 14-Across
46. Houston hockey team of the 1970s
47. Pujols is the fastest to have reached a career total of 300 of these
48. Former Nigerian capital
49. Rudely sarcastic
50. Director Oliver

Down

1. Biennial games org.
2. Couch
3. Banned apple spray
4. With 29-Across, defensive award Pujols won in 2006
5. Signed up for the Army
6. Poker prizes
7. Subdivision division
8. Closely related
9. Boy in the Dominican Republic
10. Frat party barrels
12. Come from behind in a ball game
14. Sheep's bleat
16. Born as
19. Grow older
20. Street of horror movies
21. Stick up
22. St. crosser
24. Land parts that touch other lands
25. Ben-_____ (Heston role)
26. Mama bear in Spanish
27. Mo. in which the World Series is played
28. That girl
32. Guzzles
33. Dollar divs
35. "_____ you game?"
36. Morse code bits
37. "_____ calling"

38. Actress Moore
39. Cab charge
40. Pujols' team _____ the Tigers to win the 2006 World Series
41. Golden Fleece ship
42. In the near future
43. In _____ (actually)
45. Primary team color for Pujols and the 15-Across

XOXO

Place an X or an O inside each empty cell of the grid so that there appears no row, column, or diagonal with 4 consecutive cells with the same letter.

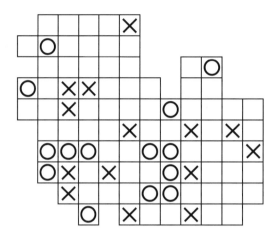

Sudoku

Use deductive logic to complete the grid so that each row, each column, and each 3 by 3 box contains the numbers 1 through 9 in some order. The solution is unique.

					3	6		
3			7	1		4		
5			8	4	6	2		
4	1			9				6
		5				1		
6				7			3	5
		3	4	8	1			7
		4		6	7			2
		6	9					

Answers on page 174.

Word Columns

Find the humorous statement by using the letters directly below each of the blank squares. Each letter is used only once. A black square indicates the end of a word.

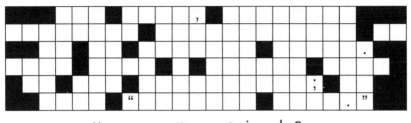

```
            u        n      s     l o
      e a   h    w i r   l n o   e d   e y
      o y o l y   n c o v i i i m e n o n d
      h s n i d e y t o w k p h g e l i t d y
    a c n Y t m e f d a i d s n g m F e d a o t e
    T o t u a l l k P r a m i l t t t b n e i t m e
```

Perfect Score

Make 3 successful hits so that the sum of the numbers is 100. Double and triple scores do not apply. Numbers may be used more than once.

Missing Connections

It's a crossword without the clues! Use the letters below to fill in the empty spaces in the crossword grid. When you are finished, you'll have words that read both across and down, crossword-style.

A A A A B B D E E E G H I L
L L N O O P R S T T T V W

Answers on page 174.

Word-a-Maze: Big Bang?

Travel in sequence through the puzzle from the left side to the right, using each numbered clue to determine the correct word. Connect adjacent words with a common letter to proceed through the maze. Some letters are already given. The first and last words tie into the title.

1. Earth, wind, and _____

2. Always

3. Prescribed ceremonies

4. Dolt

5. Final inning, typically

6. Egg-maker

7. Not southern

8. Despicable

9. Desire

10. Negative

11. Physical struggle

12. Dusk

13. Boy's club?

14. Lump

15. Put worm on hook

16. Striking

17. Toasted wafer

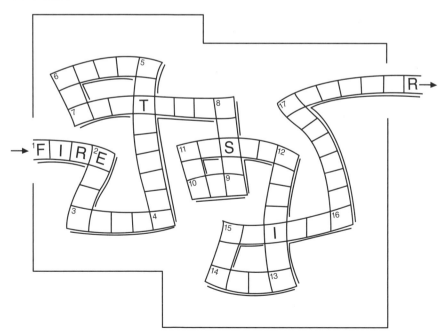

Star Power

Fill in each empty square in the grid so that each star is
surrounded by the numbers 1 through 8 with no repeats.

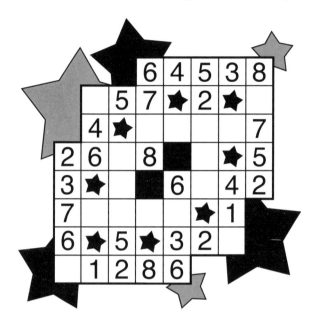

 ## Trivia on the Brain

Most people take about 6 seconds to yawn. If you see
someone yawn, there's a 55 percent chance you'll also yawn
within 5 minutes. What's funnier is that there's a 65 percent
chance you'll start yawning soon, just because you've been
reading about yawning!

Answer on page 174.

You Are Here

...and the taxi meter is ticking. This professional building is a maze of corridors and cubicles. Elevators are local or express only; there are no stairs. And over-stressed office workers won't give you directions to the exit. Why, oh why, did you ever come in here? Doesn't matter now—time to get moving!

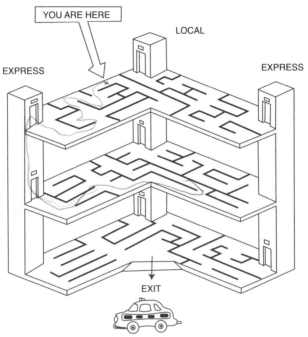

YOU ARE HERE

LOCAL

EXPRESS

EXPRESS

EXIT

Name Calling

Decipher the encoded word in the quip below using the numbers and letters on the phone pad. Remember that each number can stand for 3 or 4 possible letters.

An 3–5–3–7–4–2–6–8 is a mouse

with an operating system.

1	2 ABC	3 DEF
4 GHI	5 JKL	6 MNO
7 PQRS	8 TUV	9 WXYZ
	0	

Ripe for the Picking
by Alpha Sleuth™

Move each of the letters below into the grid to form common words. You will use each letter once. The letters in the numbered cells of the grid correspond to the letters in the phrase at the bottom. Completing the grid will help you complete the phrase and vice versa. When finished, the grid and phrase should be filled with valid words, and you will have used all the letters in the letter set.

Hint: The numbered cells in the grid are arranged alphabetically, so the letter in the cell marked 1 will appear in the alphabet before the letter in the cell marked 2, and so on.

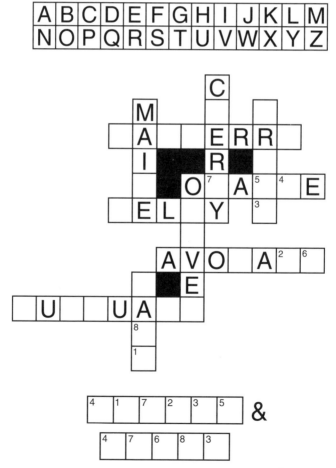

Answers on page 175.

Marbles

Place 11 marbles into the grid without having any touch one another, not even diagonally. There are some walls, represented by thick lines, that block the view of the marbles. Marbles must not "see" each other in a horizontal or vertical direction. We've placed 1 to get you started.

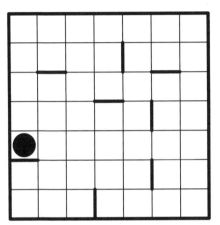

Calcu-doku

Use arithmetic and deductive logic to complete the grid so that each row and each column contains the numbers 1 through 5 in some order. Numbers in each outlined set of squares combine to produce the number in the top corner using the mathematical sign indicated.

6×		4-		8+
6+	11+	2/		
			3	
2/		15×	20×	
1-			2/	

Cast-a-Word

There are 4 dice, and there are different letters of the alphabet on the 6 faces of each of them (each letter appears only once). Random throws of the dice produced the words in this list. Can you figure out which letters appear on each of the 4 dice?

BLUE	JADE	STIR
CAGE	LAZE	TINY
CLAW	MAKE	TUNE
FAUN	QUAD	WHIM
FOIL	SLIT	VINE

Cluster

Fill in each grape so that the number in descending rows is the total of the neighboring numbers from the row above it. Each grape contains a positive whole number. Numbers can be repeated.

Answers on page 175.

Spell Math!

Spell out numbers in the blanks below to obtain the correct solution. Numbers are used only once and range from 1 to 20. A letter has been given to get you started.

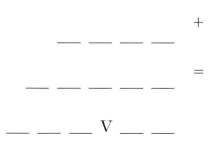

$$+$$

— — — —

$$=$$

— — — — —

— — — V — —

L'adder

Starting at the bottom rung, use the numbers 1 through 9 to add up to the top number. Numbers can only be used once. There's a catch though: The precise sums must be met along the way.

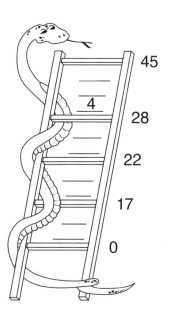

45

4

28

22

17

0

Vex-a-Gon

Place the numbers 1 through 6 into the triangles of each hexagon. The numbers may be in any order, but they do not repeat within each hexagon shape.

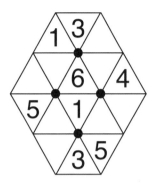

Arrow Web

Shade in some of the arrows so that each arrow in the grid points to exactly 1 shaded arrow.

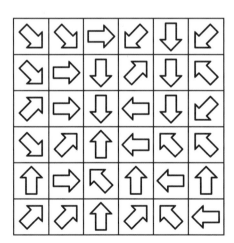

Answers on pages 175–176.

Dissection

Separate the figure into 2 identical sections following the grid lines. The sections may be rotated and/or mirrored.

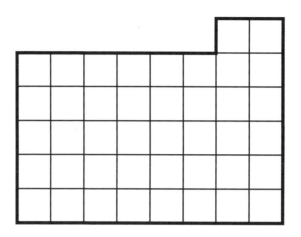

Cross Count

All the letters of the alphabet have been assigned a value from 1 through 9, as demonstrated in the box below. Fill in the grid with common English words so that the rows and columns add up correctly.

1	2	3	4	5	6	7	8	9
A	B	C	D	E	F	G	H	I
J	K	L	M	N	O	P	Q	R
S	T	U	V	W	X	Y	Z	

2			7	27
	o			24
				14
p			n	16
19	21	19	22	

CREATIVE THINKING · SPATIAL VISUALIZATION · VISUAL LOGIC · COMPUTATION · LANGUAGE

Missing Connections

It's a crossword without the clues! Use the letters below to fill in the empty spaces in the crossword grid. When you are finished, you'll have words that read both across and down, crossword-style.

A A A D D E E E E F F G K

L L M O P R R R S S T T T Y Y

Trivia on the Brain

London mapmaker John Spilsbury produced the first jigsaw puzzle in the early 1760s. He pasted a map of Britain onto a piece of wood and then cut around the counties. These jigsaw puzzles were called "dissected maps" and were used to help teach geography to kids.

Answers on page 176.

Elevator Words

Like an elevator, words move up and down the "floors" of this puzzle. Starting with the first answer, the second word from each answer carries down to become the first word of the following answer. With the clues given, complete the puzzle.

Clues

1. Star's assignment

2. One worthy of imitation

3. Early auto

4. Architect's tool

5. 3, to 9

6. Soft drink

7. Collegians' contest

1. Title _____

2. _____ _____

3. _____ _____

4. _____ _____

5. _____ _____

6. _____ _____

7. _____ Pong

Perfect Score

Make 3 successful hits so that the sum of the numbers is 100. Double and triple scores do not apply. Numbers may be used more than once.

Answers on page 176.

Change of Scenery
by Alpha Sleuth™

Move each of the letters below into the grid to form common words. You will use each letter once. The letters in the numbered cells of the grid correspond to the letters in the phrase at the bottom. Completing the grid will help you complete the phrase and vice versa. When finished, the grid and phrase should be filled with valid words, and you will have used all the letters in the letter set.

Hint: The numbered cells in the grid are arranged alphabetically, so the letter in the cell marked 1 will appear in the alphabet before the letter in the cell marked 2, and so on.

Answers on page 176.

Clone It!

Use the grid dots as a guide to split the shaded shape into 2 smaller shapes that are either identical or mirror one another.

For a hint, study the example illustrations at the bottom.

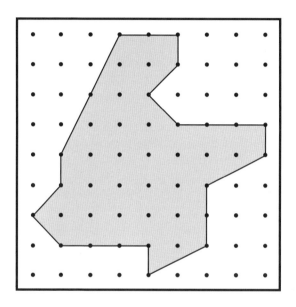

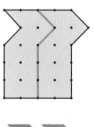

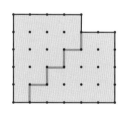

XOXO

Place an X or an O inside each empty cell of the grid so that there appears no row, column, or diagonal with 4 consecutive cells with the same letter.

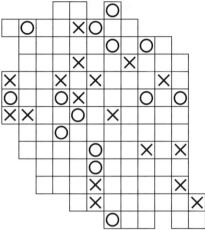

Code-doku

Solve this puzzle just as you would a sudoku. Use deductive logic to complete the grid so that each row, each column, and each 3 by 3 box contains each of the letters ADEGLNOST in some order. The solution is unique.

When you have completed the puzzle, unscramble the letters to reveal a 19th-century, Earth-friendly UK politician.

					E			
S		L	A		O	T		
D						G		L
E		S						G
	T		G	A	D		N	
N						O		A
T		D						N
		N	L		G	D		
			N					O

Answers on pages 176–177.

Word Columns

Find the hidden phrase by using the letters directly below each of the blank squares. Each letter is used only once. A black square indicates the end of a word.

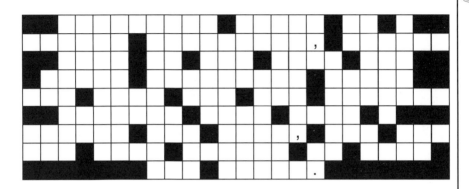

```
                  w
    o     an   n        d o e s
    t    c n   i o a y c i n k e        r   o
    t  s o h   s f s e r u o h t     y a t i e
  h p v t o   l o p n e s p n s    e o e i c
p r A h e n i y a u i m r t l e o v o u h a a
t e x l m r o p s i n o r r n y s w h a a e e y
p e e s a t e t r s w b o e n n t w n n m v l s
g e r a t t o p o g y t i o e w h o n g r e u n
```

 Trivia on the Brain

All of your "thoughts" are actually just a combination of electricity and chemicals in your brain.

Once Upon a Time...

The grid contains fairy-tale titles and characters. The words can be found in a straight line horizontally, vertically, or diagonally. They may be read either backward or forward. Leftover letters spell out an additional fact.

ALADDIN

ALI BABA

BLUEBEARD

BOY WHO CRIED WOLF

BUTTERCUP

CATSKIN

CINDERELLA

DAPPLEGRIM

FIR TREE

FROG PRINCE

GOAT GIRL

GOLDEN GOOSE

GOLDILOCKS

HANSEL AND GRETEL

KATE CRACKERNUTS

LITTLE MATCH GIRL

LITTLE RED RIDING HOOD

NUTCRACKER

PIED PIPER

PINOCCHIO

RAPUNZEL

RUMPELSTILTSKIN

SNOW WHITE

TROLL

```
L R N I D D A L A I S R F E
I U T M O S L R I G T A O G
E M L I O F I I B R U P S L
T P H R H E R G O E N U M E
O E E G G E H Y K R N S T
T L S E N C P C W C E Z W E
O S O L I N I T H A K E N R
C T O P D I P A O R C L D G
E I G P I R D M C C A R F D
U L N A R P E E R T R I F N
O T E D D G I L I U C L F A
I S D A E O P T E N E I D L
H K L R R R Y T D T T A R E
C I O L E F E I W E A S A S
C N G O L D I L O C K S E N
O A I D T H L A L I B A B A
N I K S T A C L F A A N E H
I S E T I H W W O N S C U H
P R I S L T I A N R A N L D
E R S E P U C R E T T U B N
```

Leftover letters:_____

_____

Star Power

Fill in each empty square in the grid so that each star is surrounded by the numbers 1 through 8 with no repeats.

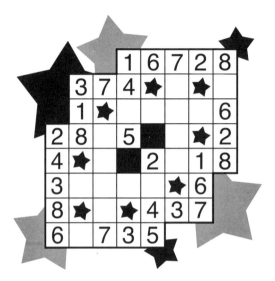

Word Jigsaw

Fit the pieces into the frame to form common, uncapitalized words reading across and down. There's no need to rotate the pieces; they'll fit as shown, with each piece used exactly once.

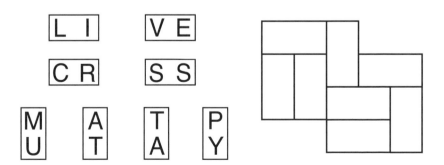

Answers on page 177.

Mr. Fix-it

Help this poor guy race through this maze, touching each of the 5 chores he has remaining so he can sit down and enjoy the big game.

Hot Parade

The weekly edition of *Hot Parade* has just been published showing the top five downloaded songs on the Internet, together with the artist. However, the copy editor has made some errors. Although each item is in the correct column, only one item in each column is correctly positioned. The following facts are true about the correct order:

1. Woodlake is not directly above or below Porthome.

2. Waterfall is 1 above McArty but 1 below Dustin.

3. Mark is 2 places below Sky.

4. Porthome is 2 places above Heaven.

5. Saul is 2 places below Woodlake.

Can you give the correct name, surname, and song for each position?

	Name	Surname	Song
1	Amy	Porthome	Yippee!
2	Saul	McArty	Heaven
3	Dustin	Woodlake	Waterfall
4	Girly	Bassett	River
5	Mark	Jakeson	Sky

Answers on page 177.

Number Crossword

Fill in this crossword with numbers instead of letters. Use the clues to determine which of the numbers 1 through 9 belongs in each square. No zeros are used.

Across

1. A square number

4. Consecutive digits, descending

6. A number in the form of abab

7. Each digit is a different multiple of 3

Down

1. Its middle digit is the sum of its 2 outside digits

2. Consecutive digits, ascending

3. The sum of its digits is 18

5. Its middle digit is the sum of its 2 outside digits

Calcu-doku

Use arithmetic and deductive logic to complete the grid so that each row and each column contains the numbers 1 through 5 in some order. Numbers in each outlined set of squares combine to produce the number in the top corner using the mathematical sign indicated.

VISUAL LOGIC
SPATIAL VISUALIZATION
CREATIVE THINKING

Uncrossed Paths

Draw lines to like symbols (triangle to triangle, star to star) without any line crossing another line. A black line cannot be crossed, while a striped line can be crossed only once.

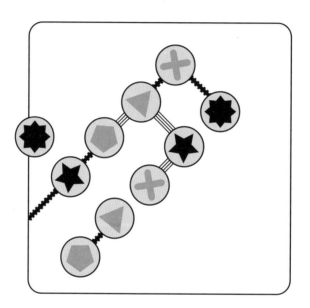

Trivia on the Brain

Did you know that 95 percent of your brain is taken up by the communication network that runs between the remaining 5 percent of grey cells?

Answer on page 178.

Word-a-Maze: Tiny Dwelling

Travel in sequence through the puzzle from the left side to the right, using each numbered clue to determine the correct word. Connect adjacent words with a common letter to proceed through the maze. Some letters are already given. The first and last words tie into the title.

1. Aircraft, informal

2. Float freely

3. Warm and sunny

4. Booty

5. Big lumber

6. Copy

7. Have fun

8. Positive

9. On your posterior

10. Indian temple

11. Very fast (slang)

12. A bother

13. To attain

14. Amphibian

15. Small amount

16. Moolah

17. Contain

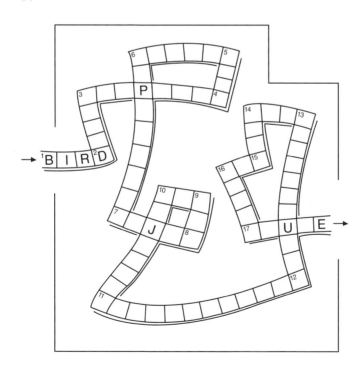

About Face

Across

1. Intended course
5. Leaf of grass
10. Practice boxing
14. No friend to Othello
15. Hammerin' Hank
16. Superman's childhood pal Lang
17. Bancroft-MacLaine film: 3 wds.
20. In order
21. Be in accord
22. Cravats
23. Marketplaces in ancient Rome
25. Riding clothes
28. Exacts
31. South Seas romance of 1847
32. Greased
33. Narrow inlet
35. Novel by John Marquand: 4 wds.
39. Spring collectors: abbr.
40. Eroded
41. "Planet of the _____"
42. Calmed with medication
44. Ancient Palestinian fortress
46. Organization: abbr.
47. Sing with great force
48. Look fixedly
51. Snakes
55. Lets the heat in: 4 wds.
58. Poker stake
59. Of space
60. Speedy animal
61. Film holder
62. "Funny Girl" Brice
63. Sea eagle

Down

1. Bread used in the East
2. The Cowardly Lion actor
3. Land in Caesar's day
4. Memo
5. Flat-bottomed boats
6. Bowling alleys
7. Parched
8. Knotts
9. School subject: abbr.
10. "I Like Ike," e.g.
11. Two of a kind
12. Bancroft or Boleyn
13. Evaluate
18. Part of a military group
19. Thanksgiving Day event
23. Wrong-doer
24. Hebrew measure
25. Mesa dwellers
26. Cupids in paintings
27. Capital of Idaho
28. Broke bread
29. Mountain dweller of Tibet
30. Begot
32. Many times
34. Handle: Lat.

36. Raises the nap
37. Fare for Dobbin
38. "_____ luxury of woe" (Thomas Moore): 2 wds.
43. Type of grass
44. Just
45. Paradise for skiers
47. Irish playwright
48. Play the lead

49. Choreographer Tommy
50. Comedian Johnson
51. British carbine
52. At hand
53. Mountain lake
54. Pintail duck
56. Blockhead
57. Gun owners group: abbr.

ANALYSIS

Name Calling

Decipher the encoded words in the quip below using the numbers and letters on the phone pad. Remember that each number can stand for 3 or 4 possible letters.

Ask about your 6–3–4–4–4–2–6–7–7, then 2–8–9 the 4–6–8–7–3.

PLANNING

LOGIC

Odd-Even Logidoku

The numbers 1 to 9 are to appear once in every row, column, long diagonal, irregular shape, and 3 by 3 grid. Cells marked with the letter **E** contain even numbers. From the numbers given, can you complete the puzzle?

Answers on page 178.

Hashi

Each circle represents an island, with the number inside indicating the number of bridges connected to it. Draw bridges between islands using the number given, but there can be no more than 2 bridges going in the same direction and there must be a continuous path connecting all islands. Bridges can only be vertical or horizontal and may not cross islands or other bridges. We've drawn some bridges to get you started.

Cast-a-Word

There are 4 dice, and there are different letters of the alphabet on the 6 faces of each of them (each letter appears only once). Random throws of the dice produced the words in this list. Can you figure out which letters appear on each of the 4 dice?

ABLE	HOME	SIZE
CLUB	LIST	STOP
COGS	PANE	VAIN
FILM	POKE	WICK
FOXY	PREY	
GOAD	RISE	

PLANNING · VISUAL LOGIC

LOGIC · PROBLEM SOLVING

Special Days and Holidays

Every word listed below is contained within this group of letters. Words can be found horizontally or vertically. They may read either backward or forward. When you have found all the words, the remaining letters will reveal 2 more special days.

ANNIVERSARY	EASTER	MAYDAY
ARBOR (Day)	GRADUATION	MEMORIAL (Day)
BIRTHDAY	HANUKKAH	NEW YEAR
CHRISTMAS	KWANZAA	THANKSGIVING
EARTH (Day)	LABOR (Day)	VETERANS (Day)

```
S  A  M  T  S  I  R  H  C  P  V  R
K  W  A  N  Z  A  A  E  S  I  E  N
D  E  Y  A  D  H  T  R  I  B  T  E
N  T  D  S  A  R  E  T  S  A  E  W
N  L  A  I  R  O  M  E  M  D  R  Y
G  R  Y  L  A  B  O  R  O  U  A  E
N  Y  R  A  S  R  E  V  I  N  N  A
G  R  A  D  U  A  T  I  O  N  S  R
G  N  I  V  I  G  S  K  N  A  H  T
D  H  O  G  H  A  K  K  U  N  A  H
```

Two more special "days": _____

Answers on page 178.

Manly Scramblegram

Four 8-letter words, all on the same theme, have been jumbled. Unscramble each word and write the answer in the accompanying space. Next, transfer the letters in the shaded boxes into the shaded keyword space and unscramble that to discover a 9-letter word that goes with the theme. The theme for this puzzle is men's names.

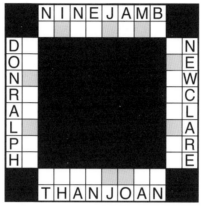

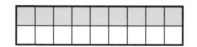

Perfect Score

Make 3 successful hits so that the sum of the numbers is 100. Double and triple scores do not apply. Numbers may be used more than once.

Answers on page 179. **95**

Arrow Web

Shade in some of the arrows so that each arrow in the grid points to exactly 1 shaded arrow.

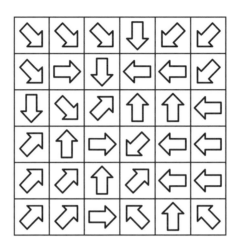

Word Ladder

Use the clues to change just one letter on each line to go from the top word to the bottom word. Do not change the order of the letters. You must have a common English word at each step.

SHELL

_____ a surface for storage or display

_____ a bundle of corn

_____ gets wool from sheep

_____ vertical drop

CHEER

Answers on page 179.

Hamster Treadmill

Only one of these exercise devices allows the hamster to run freely without the belts getting stuck. Is it device A or B?

A.

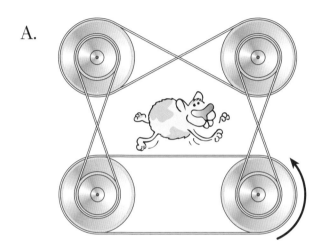

B.

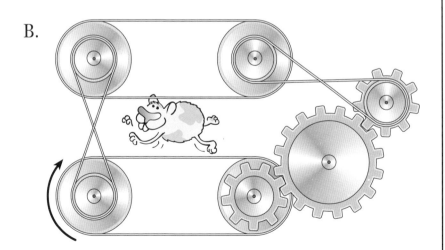

Cube Quandary

Below is an unfolded cube. Beneath it are 5 cubes that represent
what the unfolded cube would look like when formed into a cube.
One of the cubes is impossible. Can you visually determine which
one it is?

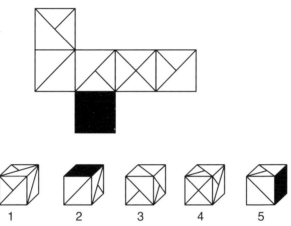

Cluster

Fill in each grape so that the number in descending rows is
the total of the neighboring numbers from the row above it.
Each grape contains a positive whole number. Numbers can be
repeated.

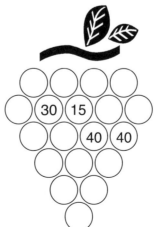

VISUAL LOGIC

SPATIAL VISUALIZATION

CREATIVE THINKING

COMPUTATION

ANALYSIS

Answers on page 179.

Hitori

The object of this puzzle is to have a number appear only once in each row and column. By shading a number cell, you are effectively removing that number from its row and column. There's a catch, though: Shaded number cells are never adjacent to one another in a row or column.

7	2	8	3	7	4	6	2
1	8	6	6	3	2	5	7
7	4	5	7	1	1	1	2
3	7	4	2	1	8	7	2
2	7	4	6	8	3	4	1
6	7	2	4	7	4	1	8
8	3	7	1	7	6	2	5
5	3	3	2	6	7	8	4

Trivia on the Brain

New research shows that the more you use a particular part of your brain, more blood is pumped to that area to provide energy. And, just as with exercising muscles, the more you use your brain the better it works.

Get It Straight

Don't get too caught up in all the twists and turns as you negotiate your way to the center of this intricate labyrinth.

Digital Sudoku

Fill in the grid so that each row, column, and 2 by 3 block contains the numbers 1 through 6 exactly once. Numbers are in digital form, and some segments have already been filled in.

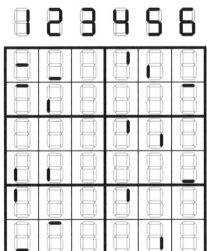

Answers on page 179.

Twisted Path

Starting from the X, draw a
continuous path that twists around all
the trees once without the path
crossing itself, though it may con-
tinue adjacent to itself. The path
should be as short as possible and
cannot pass between 2 black dots
or surround a black dot. The path
should lead you back to the X.

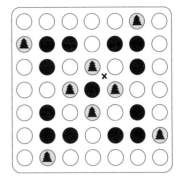

Grid Fill

To complete this puzzle, place the given letters and words into the
shapes on this grid. Words and letters will run across, down, and
wrap around each shape. When the grid is filled, each row will
contain one of the following words: alters, credit, hardly, needle,
school, snappy, streak.

1. C, D, H, L

2. ED, IT, LN, PD, PY, RS

3. ACT, ALE, ASH, ERE, ORE, SSN

4. TEAR, YOLK

Cross Count

All the letters of the alphabet have been assigned values from 1 through 9, as demonstrated in the box below. Fill in the grid with common English words so that the rows and columns add up correctly. The completed grid will contain a governmental acronym and a tennis legend.

1	2	3	4	5	6	7	8	9
A	B	C	D	E	F	G	H	I
J	K	L	M	N	O	P	Q	R
S	T	U	V	W	X	Y	Z	

			m	11
r			e	21
o			a	16
	5			22
25	15	15	15	

Vex-a-Gon

Place the numbers 1 through 6 into the triangles of each hexagon. The numbers may be in any order, but they do not repeat within each hexagon shape.

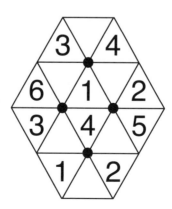

Answers on page 180.

Word Jigsaw

Fit the pieces into the frame to form common, uncapitalized words reading across and down. There's no need to rotate the pieces; they'll fit as shown, with each piece used exactly once.

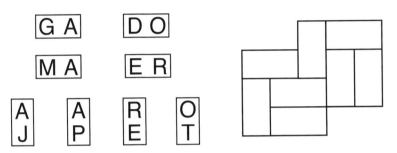

Calcu-doku

Use arithmetic and deductive logic to complete the grid so that each row and each column contains the numbers 1 through 5 in some order. Numbers in each outlined set of squares combine to produce the number in the top corner using the mathematical sign indicated.

10×		4-	1-	
36×			2/	6+
	14+			
3+			2/	
	5+		15×	

Energize the
LEVEL 4 Neuron Network
You Are Here

...and the taxi meter is ticking. This professional building is a maze of corridors and cubicles. Elevators are local or express only; there are no stairs. And over-stressed office workers won't give you directions to the exit. Why, oh why, did you ever come in here? Doesn't matter now—time to get moving!

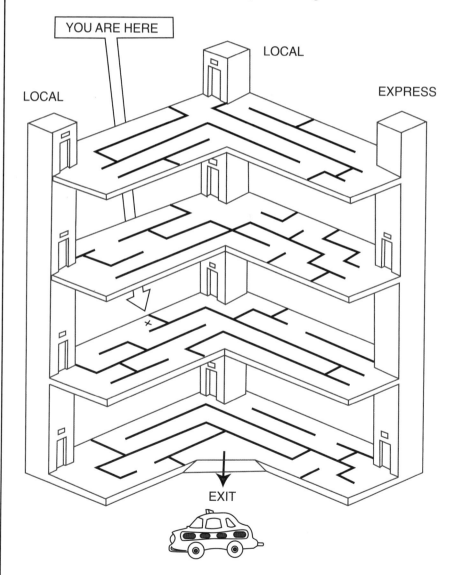

YOU ARE HERE

LOCAL

LOCAL

EXPRESS

EXIT

Answer on page 180.

Red, White, Blue, and Green

Two reds, 2 whites, 2 blues, and 2 greens are to be placed in every row, column, and long diagonal. The following clues will help you place them.

1. Each green is immediately right of each red; the blues are directly enclosed by the whites.

3. A red and a white are directly enclosed by the greens.

4. The whites are separated by 6 cells.

7. There are no blues in cells A, B, C, or D.

8. The blues are separated by 5 cells.

A. The pattern of colors takes the form abcdacbd.

C. The blues and the greens are directly enclosed by the whites.

D. Each white is immediately above each red.

E. The reds and a white are directly enclosed by the blues.

F. The whites are separated by 6 cells; the greens are adjacent.

G. Each white is immediately above each green.

H. The whites and a red are directly enclosed by the greens.

```
   A B C D E F G H
1 ┌─┬─┬─┬─┬─┬─┬─┬─┐
2 ├─┼─┼─┼─┼─┼─┼─┼─┤
3 ├─┼─┼─┼─┼─┼─┼─┼─┤
4 ├─┼─┼─┼─┼─┼─┼─┼─┤
5 ├─┼─┼─┼─┼─┼─┼─┼─┤
6 ├─┼─┼─┼─┼─┼─┼─┼─┤
7 ├─┼─┼─┼─┼─┼─┼─┼─┤
8 └─┴─┴─┴─┴─┴─┴─┴─┘
```

Answer on page 180.

1-2-3

Place the numbers 1, 2, or 3 in the circles below. The challenge is to have only these 3 numbers in each connected row and column—no number should repeat. Any combination is allowed.

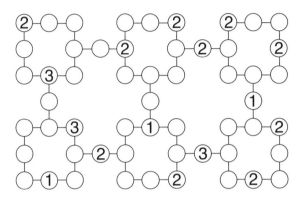

Arrow Web

Shade in some of the arrows so that each arrow in the grid points to exactly 1 shaded arrow.

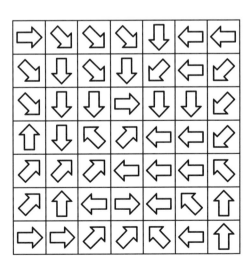

Answers on page 180.

Word-a-Maze: Car Igniter

Travel in sequence through the puzzle from the left side to the right, using each numbered clue to determine the correct word. Connect adjacent words with a common letter to proceed through the maze. Some letters are already given. The first and last words tie into the title.

1. Electricity

2. Sets of ivories

3. Grit

4. Slightly wet

5. Certain earlobes

6. Pencil art

7. "The _____ Show"

8. Elegant

9. Count on

10. Awaiting

11. Prong

12. Way out

13. Wall Street job

14. Morning greeter

15. Finger ornament

16. Sloe _____ fizz

17. Unmentionables

18. Dinner, for short

19. Sink stopper

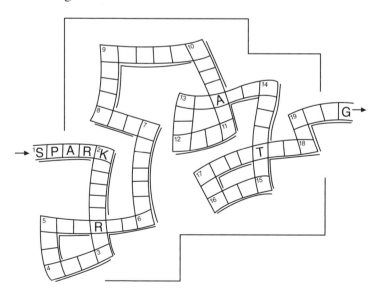

XOXO

Place an X or an O inside each empty cell of the grid so that there appears no row, column, or diagonal with 4 consecutive cells with the same letter.

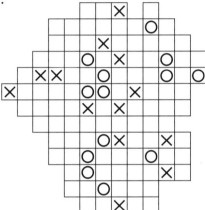

Hashi

Each circle represents an island, with the number inside indicating the number of bridges connected to it. Draw bridges between islands using the number given, but there can be no more than 2 bridges going in the same direction and there must be a continuous path connecting all islands. Bridges can only be vertical or horizontal and may not cross islands or other bridges. We've drawn some bridges to get you started.

Answers on page 181.

Perfect Score

Make 3 successful hits so that the sum of the numbers is 100. Double and triple scores do not apply. Numbers may be used more than once.

Odd-Even Logidoku

The numbers 1 to 9 are to appear once in every row, column, long diagonal, irregular shape, and 3 by 3 grid. Cells marked with the letter **E** contain even numbers. From the numbers given, can you complete the puzzle?

Uncrossed Paths

Draw lines to like symbols (triangle to triangle, star to star) without any line crossing another line. A black line cannot be crossed, a striped line can be crossed only once, and a wavy line must be crossed at least three times.

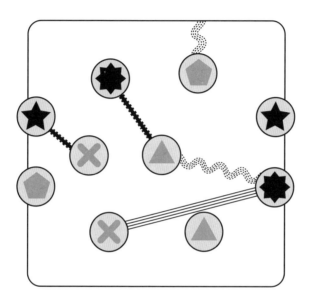

Trivia on the Brain

Getting snippets of an annoying song stuck in your head might not be fun, but sequence recall does have a useful purpose. Otherwise you wouldn't be able to autopilot everyday sequences like signing your name, repeating your phone number, or knowing the street names that come before a turn on the drive home.

Answer on page 181.

Digital Sudoku

Fill in the grid so that each row, column, and 2 by 3 block contains the numbers 1 through 6 exactly once. Numbers are in digital form, and some segments have already been filled in.

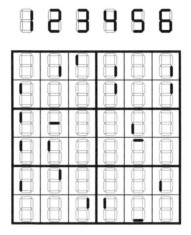

Cluster

Fill in each grape so that the number in descending rows is the total of the neighboring numbers from the row above it. Each grape contains a positive whole number. Numbers can be repeated.

Answers on page 181. **111**

Get It Straight

Don't get too caught up in all the twists and turns as you negotiate your way to the center of this intricate labyrinth.

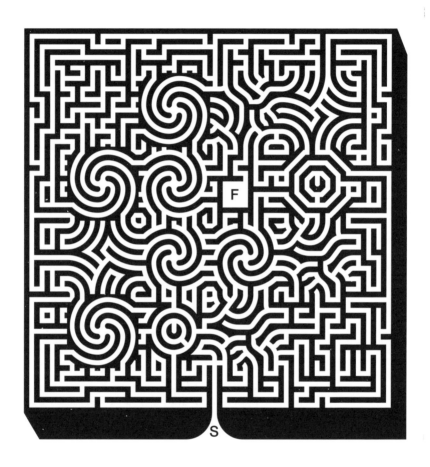

Answer on page 181.

Cross Count

All the letters of the alphabet have been assigned a value from 1 through 9, as demonstrated in the box below. Fill in the grid with common English words so that the rows and columns add up correctly.

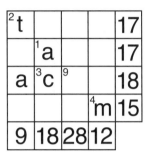

1	2	3	4	5	6	7	8	9
A	B	C	D	E	F	G	H	I
J	K	L	M	N	O	P	Q	R
S	T	U	V	W	X	Y	Z	

Calcu-doku

Use arithmetic and deductive logic to complete the grid so that each row and each column contains the numbers 1 through 6 in some order. Numbers in each outlined set of squares combine to produce the number in the top corner using the mathematical sign indicated.

6	2/		7+	2/	5
2/		10×			4+
4×	6		15+		
	2-			3+	
45×		7+		10×	2-
		8×			

Word Jigsaw

Fit the pieces into the frame to form common, uncapitalized words reading across and down. There's no need to rotate the pieces; they'll fit as shown, with each piece used exactly once.

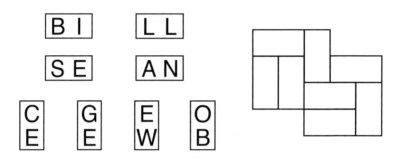

Vex-a-Gon

Place the numbers 1 through 6 into the triangles of each hexagon. The numbers may be in any order, but they do not repeat within each hexagon shape.

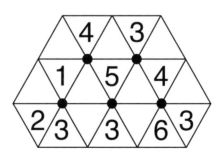

Answers on page 182.

Sudoku

Use deductive logic to complete the grid so that each row, each column, and each 3 by 3 box contains the numbers 1 through 9 in some order. The solution is unique.

2	9						8	7
						1		
				4	7			2
7		9			2			
			5		8			
			1			9		4
6			7	8				
		3						
4	1						7	3

Word Ladder

Use the clues to change just one letter on each line to go from the top word to the bottom word. Do not change the order of the letters. You must have a common English word at each step.

DARK

_____ sudden, swift movement

_____ a sweet baked product

_____ to reset scales

_____ British for wheel

PYRE

Mondrianize It!

Inspired by the artwork of Belgian artist Piet Mondrian, these puzzles consist of stars and circles. Using the checkered pattern as a guide, draw in lines so that each star is in its own square, and each circle in its own rectangle.

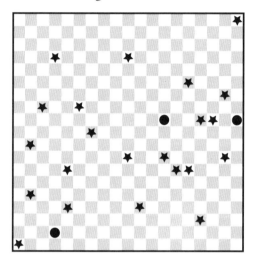

Perfect Score

Make 3 successful hits so that the sum of the numbers is 100. Double and triple scores do not apply. Numbers may be used more than once.

116

Kakuro

Place a number from 1 through 9 in each empty cell so that the sum of each vertical or horizontal run (rows and columns extending from already numbered cells) equals the number at the top or on the left of that run. Numbers may not be repeated in any run, and runs end at dark-colored squares.

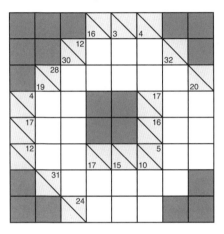

Cube Quandary

Below are 3 views of the same cube. What letter is on the face opposite (1) H, (2) X, and (3) Y?

Dance Fever

The grid on the next page contains terms associated with dances. The words can be found in a straight line horizontally, vertically, or diagonally. They may be read either backward or forward. Leftover letters spell out some additional dances.

BALBOA	DISCO	IRISH
BELLY DANCE	FANDANGO	JAZZ
BOOGIE WOOGIE	FLAMENCO	JIG
	FOLK	LINDY HOP
BREAKDANCE	FRUG	SHAG
CAKEWALK	FUNK	SHAKE
CARIOCA	GAVOTTE	SHIMMY
CASTLE WALK	HIGHLAND	TANGO
CHARLESTON	HIP HOP	TROIKA
CIRCLE	HOKEY POKEY	TWIST
CONGA	HULA	WALTZ
CONTRA	HULLY GULLY	WATUSI
COUNTRY	HUSTLE	

```
K Y M M I H S B A L L R O O M
K L B E H I G H L A N D P O C
L L A I I U E T A N G O O R A
F U O W R G O H O K H O H Y R
L G G F E I O T C P E E Y E I
A Y N D B L S O I I T B D K O
M L A O E E T H W A R T N O C
E L D Y L T W S C E O C I P A
N U N R L T S H A G I J L Y O
C H A T Y O S K K C K G H E B
O H F N D V D I E N A U O K L
C A N U A A J D W H S S T O A
S O C O N G A W A T U S I H B
I M P C C K Z T L A W L A R E
D A E F E E Z E K W M O A R E
```

Leftover letters: _____

_____

Masyu

Masyu has a simple goal: to draw a single, nonintersecting loop through all of the pearls on the grid.

There are 2 rules according to the color of the pearl:

Black pearls: A line must enter and exit at right angles from the pearl. It must also extend straight for 2 squares in the chosen direction.

White pearls: A line goes straight through each pearl and must turn immediately before or after. It is optional for the line to turn both before and after.

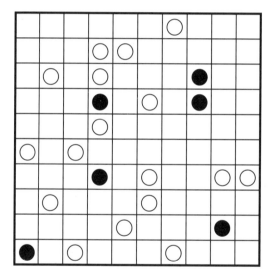

Trivia on the Brain

People tend to forget easier than they remember, which is why repetition helps things stick in your mind.

Answer on page 182.

Hamster Treadmill

When the hamster starts running on the treadmill, will the hand of the speedometer turn clockwise or counter-clockwise?

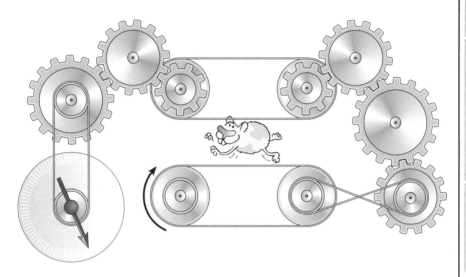

Star Power

Fill in each empty square in the grid so that each star is surrounded by the numbers 1 through 8 with no repeats.

Digital Sudoku

Fill in the grid so that each row, column, and 2 by 3 block contains the numbers 1 through 6 exactly once. Numbers are in digital form, and some segments have already been filled in.

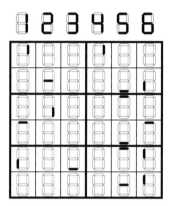

Word Columns

Find the hidden humorous anecdote by using the letters directly below each of the blank squares. Each letter is used only once. A black square indicates the end of a word.

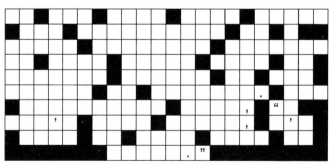

```
      n        a l t   s
    t  o l    i u o T o o     e        a
    d n e e  t s p e o c k d y h       i e
    d i c i l e k r m i r t d e s c o    a t
    a h s a p d t n h r r o n n n n t o m  l n
    s o a t t d e c c w y i r r r m o p h k n
    A n i t e a t l n d s r o o a s o f s a r y
    i o t v q r y o i c u l h g i n t o p e h e
    l f h s h u i f o a k m a a c t i a l T d d
```

Answers on page 183.

Cast-a-Word

There are 4 dice, and there are different letters of the alphabet on the 6 faces of each of them (each letter appears only once). Random throws of the dice produced the words in this list. Can you figure out which letters appear on each of the 4 dice?

COLA	GULP	PHEW
DOCK	HEWN	RUBY
DOZE	LAME	SARI
FLAT	LOUD	WIRE
FLEX	NAVY	

Marbles

Place 11 marbles into the grid without having any touch one another, not even diagonally. There are some walls, represented by thick lines, that block the view of the marbles. Marbles must not "see" each other in a horizontal or vertical direction. We've placed 1 to get you started.

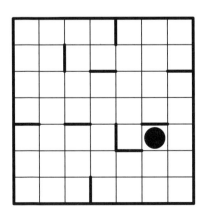

Name Calling

Decipher the encoded words in the proverb below using the
numbers and letters on the phone pad. Remember that each
number can stand for 3 or 4 possible letters.

Man should 5–4–8–3 if only to 7–2–8–4–7–3–9 his

2–8–7–4–6–7–4–8–9.

Hitori

The object of this puzzle is to have a number appear only once in
each row and column. By shading a number cell, you are effectively removing that number from its row and column. There's
a catch, though: Shaded number cells are never adjacent to one
another in a row or column.

4	6	4	5	3	8	5	2
6	7	1	2	5	2	4	6
6	3	2	5	8	4	1	7
6	4	8	6	4	3	2	3
3	2	4	5	7	1	2	5
2	3	3	7	1	3	5	8
5	1	5	4	6	7	8	3
1	6	6	3	4	5	7	2

Answers on page 183.

The Friendly Skies
by Alpha Sleuth™

Move each of the letters below into the grid to form common words. You will use each letter once. The letters in the numbered cells of the grid correspond to the letters in the phrase at the bottom. Completing the grid will help you complete the phrase and vice versa. When finished, the grid and phrase should be filled with valid words, and you will have used all the letters in the letter set.

Hint: The numbered cells in the grid are arranged alphabetically, so the letter in the cell marked 1 will appear in the alphabet before the letter in the cell marked 2, and so on.

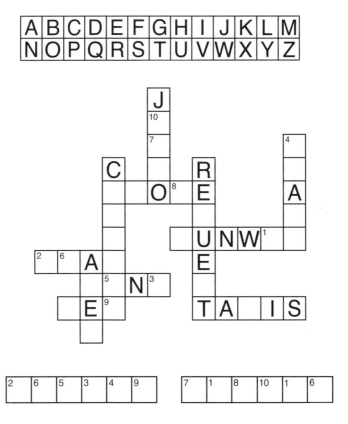

Elevator Words

Like an elevator, words move up and down the "floors" of this puzzle. Starting with the first answer, the second word from each answer carries down to become the first word of the following answer. With the clues given, complete the puzzle.

1. Minute _____

2. _____ _____

3. _____ _____

4. _____ _____

5. _____ _____

6. _____ _____

7. _____ Bearing

Clues

1. Part of a corporation's records

2. Readers' group

3. It may be made medium

4. Place to get last entry

5. Oil- or water-based purchase

6. It may be used to apply previous entry

7. Machine part

Answers on page 183.

Hashi

Each circle represents an island, with the number inside indicating the number of bridges connected to it. Draw bridges between islands using the number given, but there can be no more than 2 bridges going in the same direction and there must be a continuous path connecting all islands. Bridges can only be vertical or horizontal and may not cross islands or other bridges. We've drawn some bridges to get you started.

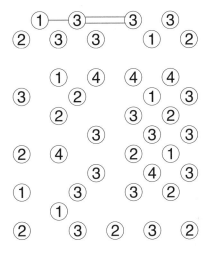

Twenty-four Jumble

Arrange the numbers and math signs in this cornucopia to come up with the number 24.

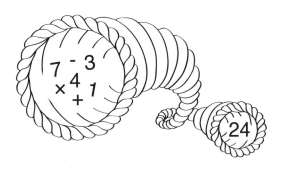

PLANNING

VISUAL LOGIC

ANALYSIS

COMPUTATION

XOXO

Place an X or an O inside each empty cell of the grid so that there appears no row, column, or diagonal with 4 consecutive cells with the same letter.

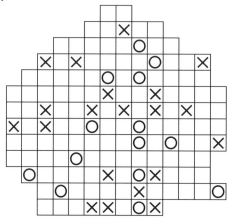

Cross Count

All the letters of the alphabet have been assigned values from 1 through 9, as demonstrated in the box below. Fill in the grid with common English words so that the rows and columns add up correctly. The completed grid will contain the Latin name of a constellation.

1	2	3	4	5	6	7	8	9
A	B	C	D	E	F	G	H	I
J	K	L	M	N	O	P	Q	R
S	T	U	V	W	X	Y	Z	

h	1			12
	9			14
	5			18
	1			14
22	16	13	7	

Answers on page 184.

The Rumor Mill by Alpha Sleuth™

Move each of the letters below into the grid to form common words. You will use each letter once. The letters in the numbered cells of the grid correspond to the letters in the phrase at the bottom. Completing the grid will help you complete the phrase and vice versa. When finished, the grid and phrase should be filled with valid words, and you will have used all the letters in the letter set.

Hint: The numbered cells in the grid are arranged alphabetically, so the letter in the cell marked 1 will appear in the alphabet before the letter in the cell marked 2, and so on.

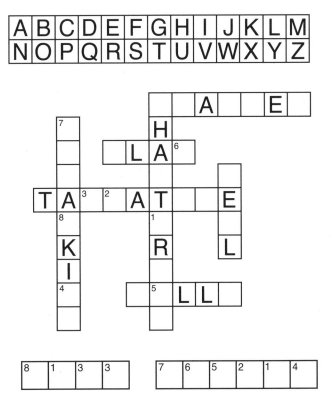

The Crossword Without a Theme

Across

1. Almost closed
5. Caviar source
8. Stringed instrument
12. The skin manufactures it when exposed to sunlight
14. About
15. As an asset
17. V followers
18. Gent
19. Offerer of moral lessons
20. Cook in the microwave, slangily
21. Summer center?
22. Mock
25. City vehicle
26. Solver's exclamation
29. Historic section of New Orleans
33. Beer container
34. British ending?
35. Slender amphibian
36. Cause perplexity in
37. Passats, e.g.
39. Tenochtitlan dweller
42. Forest mom
43. _____ Olivos, California
46. Contributed, as a comment
49. Longtime smoker?

50. Yogurt content
51. Speaks
52. Athlete's week off, perhaps
53. Big celebration

Down

1. Confess
2. Cause of bad luck
3. Part of D.A.: abbr.
4. Enthusiastic cheer
5. Shred
6. Just
7. End of Juilliard's e-mail address
8. Firefighting equipment
9. Budget competitor
10. Make over
11. Kind of school
13. _____ Millions (lottery game)
16. Brazilian dance
20. Type of meditation
21. _____ de parfum
22. Home airport of JetBlue
23. "Where the Wild Things _____" (Sendak book)
24. Categorize
25. International distress signal
26. Attacked a hero, say

27. Attack with an ax
28. Exhibit material
30. Native of Bohemia
31. Cause of bad luck
32. M.D.'s coworkers
36. Old Robert Urich
    TV series
37. Able to produce sounds
38. Traveled
39. Bowls over

40. Greek letter
41. Very little
42. Climax of the Allied
    advance
43. Mussolini's money
44. R&B singer Redding
45. Former monarch of Iran
47. Kind of tide
48. Complex arrangement

Fences

Connect the dots and draw a continuous path that doesn't cross itself. Numbers represent the "fences" created by the path (2 edges are created around the number 2, 3 edges around 3, etc.). We've started the puzzle for you.

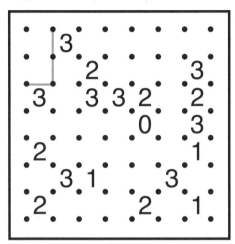

Logidoku

The numbers 1 to 9 are to be placed once in every row, column, long diagonal, irregular shape, and 3 by 3 grid. From the numbers given, can you complete the puzzle?

Answers on page 184.

Star Power

Fill in each empty square in the grid so that each star is surrounded by the numbers 1 through 8 with no repeats.

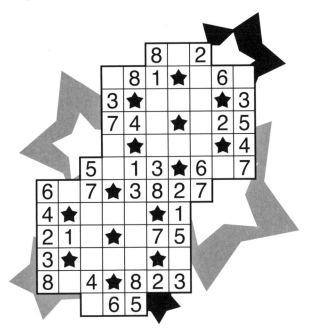

Trivia on the Brain

It takes only 10 seconds for someone to lose consciousness once blood flow is blocked from the brain.

Clone It!

Use the grid dots as a guide to split the shaded shape into 2 smaller shapes that are either identical or mirror one another.

For a hint, study the example illustrations at the bottom.

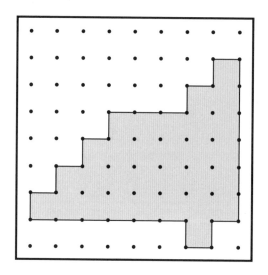

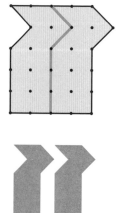

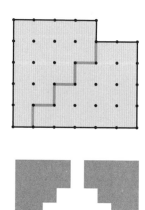

Answer on page 184.

Calcu-doku

Use arithmetic and deductive logic to complete the grid so that each row and each column contains the numbers 1 through 6 in some order. Numbers in each outlined set of squares combine to produce the number in the top corner using the mathematical sign indicated.

15×		8+	4	7+	
2/	6			4	2-
	5-		3	5+	
30×		6+			3/
	7+		30×	1	
6+				20×	

Word Columns

Find the hidden phrase by Doug Horton by using the letters directly below each of the blank squares. Each letter is used only once. A black square indicates the end of a word.

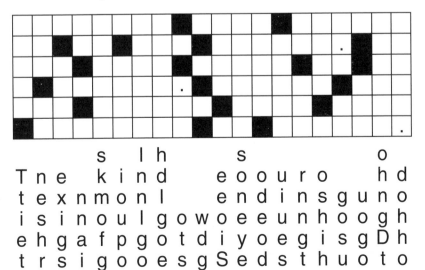

```
        s   l h       s               o
T n e   k i n d     e o o u r o       h d
t e x n m o n l     e n d i n s g u n o
i s i n o u l g o w o e e u n h o o g h
e h g a f p g o t d i y o e g i s g D h
t r s i g o o e s g S e d s t h u o t o
```

PLANNING

CREATIVE THINKING

LOGIC

ANALYSIS

Vex-a-Gon

Place the numbers 1 through 6 into the triangles of each hexagon. The numbers may be in any order, but they do not repeat within each hexagon shape.

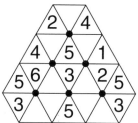

Identity Parade

Mrs. Amnesia was asked to recollect the faces of the 4 suspects who robbed the local bank. Her memory is a bit shaky though. The photos accidentally got put through a shredder, and, currently, only 1 facial feature in each row is in its correct place. Mrs. Amnesia does know that:

1. B's nose is not next to C's nose.

2. B's hair is 1 place to the right of B's nose.

3. B's eyes are 1 place to the right of B's mouth.

4. A's hair is 1 place to the left of D's mouth.

5. B's eyes are not on the same face as C's nose.

6. C's eyes are 1 place to the left of C's nose.

Can you find the correct hair, eyes, nose, and mouth for each suspect?

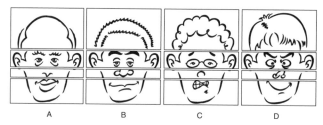

A   B   C   D

Answers on page 185.

LEVEL 5 Go the Distance!

The Straight & Narrow
by Alpha Sleuth™

Move each of the letters below into the grid to form common words. You will use each letter only once. The letters in the numbered cells of the grid correspond to the letters in the phrase at the bottom. Completing the grid will help you complete the phrase and vice versa. When finished, the grid and phrase should be filled with valid words, and you will have used all the letters in the letter set.

Hint: The numbered cells in the grid are arranged alphabetically, so the letter in the cell marked 1 will appear in the alphabet before the letter in the cell marked 2, and so on.

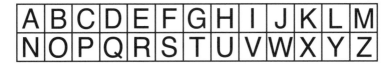

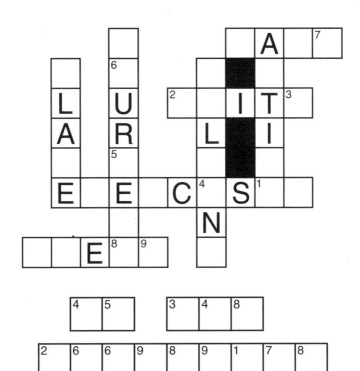

VISUAL SEARCH

ATTENTION

Swarm of **S**'s

We count 19 things in this picture that begin with the letter **S**. How many can you find?

PLANNING

LOGIC

Logidoku

The numbers 1 to 9 are to be placed once in every row, column, long diagonal, irregular shape, and 3 by 3 grid. From the numbers given, can you complete the puzzle?

	7			1				
2								
		6						8
					7			
				2				
						9		
	5							
							9	
	1			8				3

Answers on page 185.

Word Ladder

Change just one letter on each line to go from the top word to the bottom word. Each line will contain a new word. Do not change the order of the letters.

TINY

_____

_____

_____

_____

_____

HUGE

Perfect Score

Make 3 successful hits so that the sum of the numbers is 100. Double and triple scores do not apply. Numbers may be used more than once.

Red, White, Blue, and Green

Two reds, 2 whites, 2 blues, and 2 greens are to be placed in every row, column, and long diagonal. The following clues will help you place them.

1. Each red is immediately left of each blue.

2. Each white is immediately left of each green.

3. The greens, the blues, and a red are directly enclosed by the whites.

4. The pattern of colors takes the form abcbcdad.

5. Each blue is immediately right of each white.

6. The greens, the reds, and a blue are directly enclosed by the whites.

7. The blues are separated by 5 cells; each red is immediately right of each green.

A. Three different colors are directly enclosed by the whites.

B. Three different colors are directly enclosed by the blues.

F. The reds are directly enclosed by a white and a blue.

G. The reds and a blue are directly enclosed by the greens.

H. The whites cannot be found in cells 1, 2, 3, or 4.

A B C D E F G H

	A	B	C	D	E	F	G	H
1								
2								
3								
4								
5								
6								
7								
8								

Answer on page 185.

XOXO

Place an X or an O inside each empty cell of the grid so that there appears no row, column, or diagonal with 4 consecutive cells with the same letter.

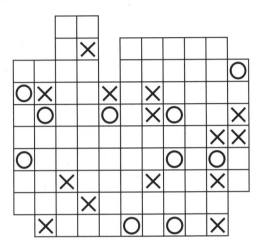

Spell Math!

Spell out numbers in the blanks below to obtain the correct solution. Numbers are used only once and range from 1 to 20.

$$\underline{}\ \underline{}\ \underline{}\ \underline{}\ \underline{}\ +$$

$$\underline{}\ \underline{}\ \underline{}\ \underline{}\ \underline{}\ \underline{}\ =$$

$$\underline{}\ \underline{}\ \underline{}\ \underline{}\ \underline{}\ \underline{}$$

LANGUAGE

GENERAL KNOWLEDGE

The Whole Shebang

Across

1. "_____ old cowhand..."
5. Dove competitor
10. Advertising award
14. _____ me tangere (touch-me-not)
15. Wear away
16. Popular spaghetti sauce brand
17. Bawdy jokes after the game, say
20. Consecrate with oil
21. _____ Digest
22. Earp of the Old West
23. Twerp
25. Island in the Firth of Clyde
27. Stones
31. Lip-reading alternative: abbr.
34. Scrambled dish
36. Goddess of the hunt
37. Investment collections
41. Saint Anthony of _____
42. _____ a soul (no one)
43. To the _____ degree
44. Look of disdain
45. Salome's seven
48. Kidney-shaped nut
51. "_____ Ike" (1950s campaign slogan)
55. Movie house
58. Ribs
59. "More fun than a _____!"
62. Saharan

63. Betelgeuse, for one
64. Really wide shoe size
65. AAA recommendations: abbr.
66. Broad neck scarf
67. Fresh remark

Down

1. Spouse's mom, e.g.
2. Lost in reverie, slangily
3. Big name in aluminum
4. Mr. Khrushchev
5. Individual breath mint
6. Part of E.T.A.: abbr.
7. Bossy remark?
8. Worship
9. Aden's land
10. Unrefined petroleum
11. Using a cane, maybe
12. Borodin's Prince
13. Belonging to us
18. _____'acte
19. Pageboy or French twist
23. Child's four-wheeler
24. Write on a ring, e.g.
26. Agent, briefly
28. Abel's brother
29. Nautical mile
30. Ornamental waistband
31. Egyptian vipers
32. Laurel or Musial
33. Rich source, as of ore
35. Scatter
38. Teleprompter's alternatives

39. A martial art
40. Post-it note abbr.
46. Security, as on a property
47. Quenches, as a thirst
49. 1965 Alabama march site
50. Perot of politics
52. "_____ long life ahead of you..." (palm reader's comment)

53. "Flowers for Algernon" author Daniel
54. Curvy characters
55. Skier's lift
56. Hind's mate
57. Buffalo's lake
58. Wrongful act, in law
60. U.S. commerce watchdog
61. Red Chairman

PLANNING | SPATIAL REASONING

Get It Straight

Don't get too caught up in all the twists and turns as you negotiate your way to the center of this intricate labyrinth.

Trivia on the Brain

What creature has the largest brain proportionally to their size? An elephant? A human? A whale? The answer is an ant! Its brain is about 6 percent of its total body weight. If we applied the same percentage to humans, our heads would have to be about 3 times as large.

Answer on page 186.

1-2-3

Place the numbers 1, 2, or 3 in the circles below. The challenge is to have only these 3 numbers in each connected row and column—no number should repeat. Any combination is allowed.

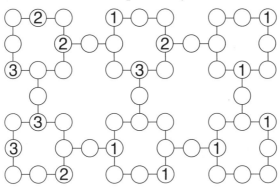

Sudoku

Use deductive logic to complete the grid so that each row, each column, and each 3 by 3 box contains the numbers 1 through 9 in some order. The solution is unique.

					2	5	6	4
			5	1				
						2		9
	6	2			3	8		
				9				
		9	7			6	3	
8		6						
				6	1			
7	5	1	8					

Kakuro

Place a number from 1 through 9 in each empty cell so that the sum of each vertical or horizontal run (rows and columns extending from already numbered cells) equals the number at the top or on the left of that run. Numbers may not be repeated in any run, and runs end at dark-colored squares.

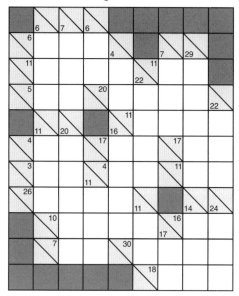

Marbles

Place 13 marbles into the grid without having any touch one another, not even diagonally. There are some walls, represented by thick lines, that block the view of the marbles. Marbles must not "see" each other in a horizontal or vertical direction. We've placed 1 to get you started.

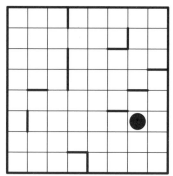

Answers on page 186.

Gridiron Prizes

The organizers of pro football's annual awards banquet have the winners and their details in the wrong order. Although the list shown has each item in the correct column, only 1 item is correctly positioned in each column. The following facts are certain about the correct order:

1. The quarterback is 1 place above Lump.

2. The slotback is 3 places below Dogger and 2 below the Beckonheres.

3. Forrester is 2 places above Gazelle and 1 below the Toxins.

4. The Irklands are 3 places above Baz.

5. Eddie is 2 places below Idle and 1 above the center.

6. The wingback is 1 place above the Stoolers and 3 above Hitman.

Can you determine the correct name, surname, position, and team name for each ranked player?

	Name	Surname	Position	Team
1	Abel	Gazelle	Center	Stoolers
2	Baz	Hitman	Fullback	Toxins
3	Chris	Idle	Wingback	Irklands
4	Dogger	Jogger	Slotback	48ers
5	Eddie	Keen	Quarterback	Wishingtan
6	Forrester	Lump	Running back	Beckonheres

Star Power

Fill in each empty square in the grid so that each star is surrounded by the numbers 1 through 8 with no repeats.

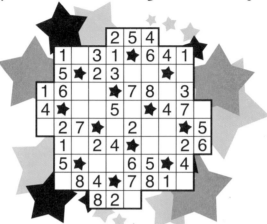

Word Columns

Find the hidden observation by using the letters directly below each of the blank squares. Each letter is used only once. A black square indicates a space between words unless the word ends at the end of a row.

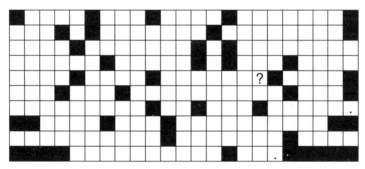

Answers on pages 186–187.

Word-a-Maze: Choppers

Travel in sequence through the puzzle from the left side to the right, using each numbered clue to determine the correct word. Connect adjacent words with a common letter to proceed through the maze. Some letters are already given. The first and last words tie into the title.

1. Not true

2. Run-away marriage

3. _____ the Cat

4. "_____ bees"

5. Critique

6. Married

7. Club cash

8. One after another

9. Hit ABC show

10. Chubby Checker dance

11. Hiding place

12. Dough riser

13. Ike _____

14. Mean and tenacious

15. Sibling

16. Booze measure

17. Molars

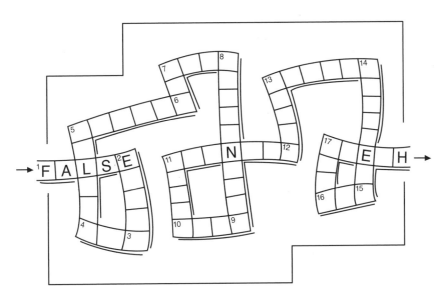

VISUAL LOGIC

SPATIAL VISUALIZATION

CREATIVE THINKING

Clone It!

Use the grid dots as a guide to split the shaded shape into 2 smaller shapes that are either identical or mirror one another.

For a hint, study the example illustrations at the bottom.

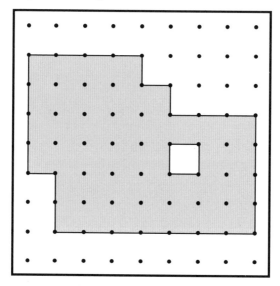

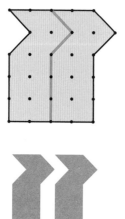

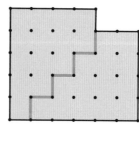

Answer on page 187.

Calcu-doku

COMPUTATION LOGIC

Use arithmetic and deductive logic to complete the grid so that each row and each column contains the numbers 1 through 6 in some order. Numbers in each outlined set of squares combine to produce the number in the top corner using the mathematical sign indicated.

7+	15×	7+		5-	
		13+	4×		6
5+			20×		12×
12×				3×	
2/		10+			10×
	5+		2-		

Digital Sudoku

LOGIC

Fill in the grid so that each row, column, and 2 by 3 block contains the numbers 1 through 6 exactly once. Numbers are in digital form, and some segments have already been filled in.

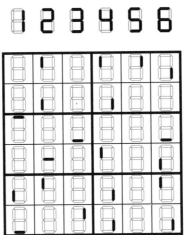

CREATIVE THINKING | PLANNING

Vex-a-Gon

Place the numbers 1 through 6 into the triangles of each hexagon. The numbers may be in any order, but they do not repeat within each hexagon shape.

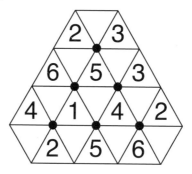

XOXO

Place an X or an O inside each empty cell of the grid so that there appears no row, column, or diagonal with 4 consecutive cells with the same letter.

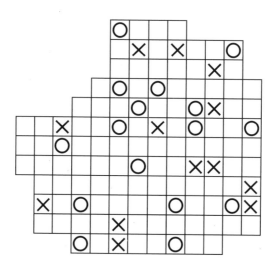

ANALYSIS | VISUAL LOGIC

152

Answers on page 187.

We'll Be A-MAZEd

...if you can make your way through this diabolical labyrinth in less than 5 minutes. Start at top left. You can go under bridges.

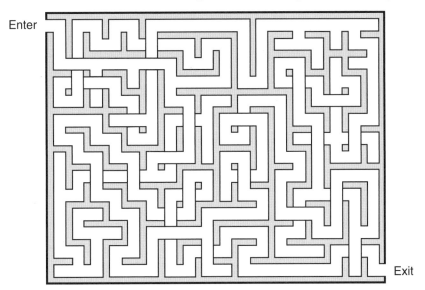

Enter

Exit

City Down Under

There's a pattern to the columns of letters below. Can you discover what the pattern is and name the famous city?

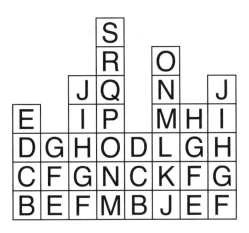

Hashi

Each circle represents an island, with the number inside indicating the number of bridges connected to it. Draw bridges between islands using the number given, but there can be no more than 2 bridges going in the same direction and there must be a continuous path connecting all islands. Bridges can only be vertical or horizontal and may not cross islands or other bridges. We've drawn some bridges to get you started.

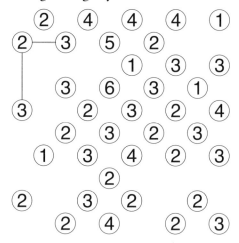

Cross Count

All the letters of the alphabet have been assigned values from 1 through 9, as demonstrated in the box below. Fill in the grid with common English words so that the rows and columns add up correctly.

1	2	3	4	5	6	7	8	9
A	B	C	D	E	F	G	H	I
J	K	L	M	N	O	P	Q	R
S	T	U	V	W	X	Y	Z	

9		p	1	21
		1		13
	9	9		28
9				23
26	24	22	13	

Answers on pages 187–188.

Logidoku

The numbers 1 to 9 are to be placed once in every row, column, long diagonal, irregular shape, and 3 by 3 grid. From the numbers given, can you complete the puzzle?

	3							
8		5		7			9	
					1			
		6						4
2		4						
					6			
	1							7

Trivia on the Brain

Just like some people need a harder physical workout than others, some need a harder mental workout, too. So, in addition to working these puzzles, try brushing your teeth or eating a bowl of cereal with the opposite hand. Or take up a new hobby that puts fine-motor skills to work, such as painting, sewing, or playing an instrument.

Fences

Connect the dots and draw a continuous path that doesn't cross itself. Numbers represent the "fences" created by the path (2 edges are created around the number 2, 3 edges around 3, etc.). We've started the puzzle for you.

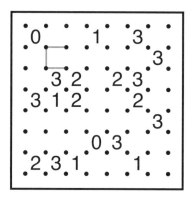

Word Jigsaw

Fit the pieces into the frame to form common, uncapitalized words reading across and down. There's no need to rotate the pieces; they'll fit as shown, with each piece used exactly once.

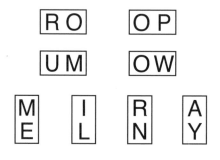

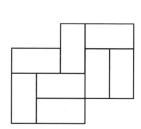

Answers on page 188.

Uncrossed Paths

Draw lines to like symbols (triangle to triangle, star to star) without any line crossing another line. A black line cannot be crossed, a striped line can be crossed only once, and a wavy line must be crossed at least three times.

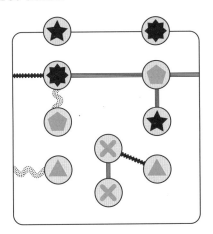

Identity Parade

Oops! Four mugshots accidentally got sent through the shredder, and Officer Wallers is trying to straighten them out. Currently, only one facial feature in each row is in its correct place. Officer Wallers knows that:

1. C's nose is 1 place to the right of her mouth and 2 places to the right of D's hair.

2. C's eyes are 2 places to the left of her hair.

3. A's eyes are 1 place to the right of B's nose and 1 place to the right of D's mouth.

Can you find the correct hair, eyes, nose, and mouth for each suspect?

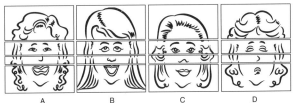

A   B   C   D

This One Will Floor You

Across

1. Barely made, with "out"
5. Chronological records of events
11. Saturn's wife
14. Kid's block
15. Yogi's pal
16. Second Amendment rights grp.
17. Good luck expression
19. The L in "L.A."
20. Instant lawn
21. They sound the same
23. Scene stealer
26. Legend in soccer
28. Short-sighted one
29. Actor Morales of "Caprica"
31. Mother of Isaac
34. They're used for blowups: abbr.
35. NCOs: abbr.
37. El Al destination
39. Enliven
41. Endurance
44. Two-deck card game
46. Pavarotti, for one
47. Like a delicate handkerchief
49. Pile
51. Word heard on New Year's Eve
52. Addis ___, Ethiopia
54. Retain
56. Poetic meadow
57. Nabbed one

60. Sushi item
62. Opening
63. Dancing, idiomatically
68. Holland city
69. Stick (to)
70. Optimistic
71. Receiving a pension, maybe: abbr.
72. Wrote, as a letter
73. Judge

Down

1. Benevolent Order member
2. Barbie's beau
3. Prima donna problem
4. AMA members
5. Homes
6. Vote in Quebec
7. The boondocks
8. "Peek" ending
9. Weaver's tool
10. City in Genesis
11. Old record collector's stipulation
12. On time
13. Gives lip
18. Keystone movie character
22. Big Apple daily, briefly
23. "_____ Rebel" (1962 pop hit)
24. Professional org.
25. Aladdin's "vehicle"
27. Most recent
30. "Quite possibly"
32. Lorraine's neighbor

33. Panama or fedora
36. _____ Diego
38. Wine tub
40. Prof's helpers, briefly
42. Not any
43. Geometric calculation
45. "Break time!"
47. Defensive encampment circled by armed vehicles
48. Use a rasp on

50. Lamented loudly
53. Music maker's org.
55. Cribbage insert
58. Arrogance in the 'hood
59. People: prefix
61. Hog fat
64. Wrath
65. Lobster eggs
66. Put into service
67. Basketball practice milieu

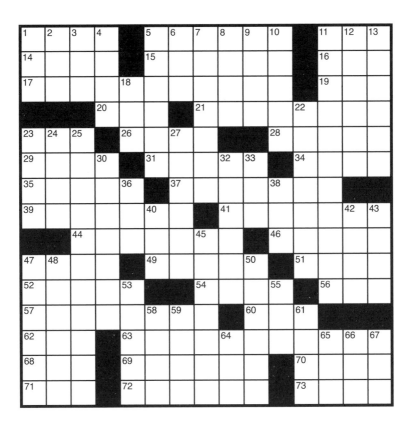

Elevator Words

Like an elevator, words move up and down the "floors" of this puzzle. Starting with the first answer, the second word from each answer carries down to become the first word of the following answer. With the clues given, complete the puzzle.

1. Amazing _____

2. _____ _____

3. _____ _____

4. _____ _____

5. _____ _____

6. _____ _____

7. _____ Wine

Clues

1. Oft sung hymn

2. She married Rainier III in 1956

3. Color worn on St. Paddy's Day

4. Environmental organization founded in Vancouver in 1971

5. It brings an end to hostilities

6. Cities opened to foreign trade in the 1800s

7. Dessert alternative or addition

Answers on page 188.

Calcu-doku

Use arithmetic and deductive logic to complete the grid so that each row and each column contains the numbers 1 through 6 in some order. Numbers in each outlined set of squares combine to produce the number in the top corner using the mathematical sign indicated.

15x		4x	8x		9+
3/			12x	6+	
5x	18x				20x
	2-	30x		12x	
2/					2/
	4+		1-		

Spell Math!

Spell out numbers in the blanks below to obtain the correct solution. Numbers are used only once and range from 1 to 20.

$$\underline{}\ \underline{}\ \underline{}\ \underline{}\ \underline{} \quad +$$

$$\underline{}\ \underline{}\ \underline{}\ \underline{}\ \underline{}\ \underline{}\ \underline{} \quad =$$

$$\underline{}\ \underline{}\ \underline{}\ \underline{}\ \underline{}\ \underline{}$$

Answers on page 188.

Name Calling

Decipher the encoded word in the quip below using the numbers and letters on the phone pad. Remember that each number can stand for 3 or 4 possible letters.

It's kind of fun to do the 4–6–7–6–7–7–4–2–5–3.

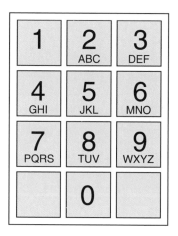

Cluster

Fill in each grape so that the number in descending rows is the total of the neighboring numbers from the row above it. Each grape contains a positive whole number. Numbers can be repeated.

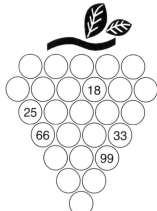

Answers on pages 188–189.

1-2-3

Place the numbers 1, 2, or 3 in the circles below. The challenge is to have only these 3 numbers in each connected row and column—no number should repeat. Any combination is allowed.

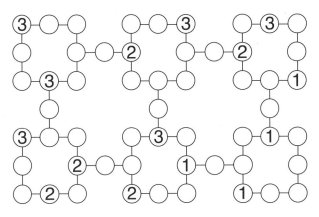

Perfect Score

Make 3 successful hits so that the sum of the numbers is 100. Double and triple scores do not apply. Numbers may be used more than once.

LOGIC PLANNING

COMPUTATION VISUAL LOGIC

Symbol Value

Can you replace the symbols with number values so that the sum of each row and column and the one diagonal add up to the number at the end of each?

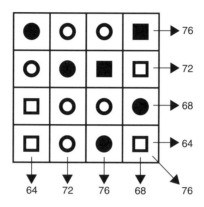

Twenty-four Jumble

Arrange the numbers and math signs in this cornucopia to come up with the number 24.

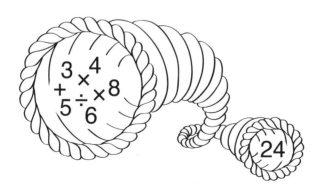

Answers on page 189.

Answers

Name Calling (page 6)

A whole fool is half a prophet.

Quic-Kross (page 6)

POTATO

You Are Here (page 7)

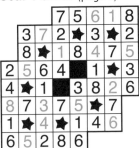

A Puzzling Perspective (page 7)

tentatively

Star Power (page 8)

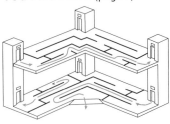

Spell Math! (page 8)

One + sixteen = seventeen

Word Jigsaw (page 9)

Perfect Score (page 10)

50 + 41 + 9 = 100

1-2-3 (page 10)

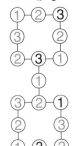

Natural Disasters

(page 11)

```
I N E H C N A L A V A T H E
L A S T D E O C A D E T H E
A V E P R B L I Z Z A R D A
M U D F L O W G T R E A N N
M E E U A A L D E P A A T H
T R N O L L G F R O U H M D
I S O I E K A U Q H T R A E
A S L T M C I M E D I P E L
T E C R S A N D S T O R M S
W A Y S A L F T H G U O R D
B O C U E D I L S D N A L T
S I X T Y S E A V E N T H F
O E V A W T A E H U S A N D
```

Leftover letters read: In the last decade the average annual death toll from disasters was about sixty seven thousand.

XOXO (page 12)

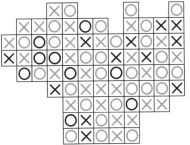

Word Ladder (page 12)

TWO, too, ton, ion, inn, ink, irk, ARK

Answers

NASCAR Weekend by Alpha Sleuth™ (page 13)

```
        I       S
        N     H A Z A R D
        F     I
    Q U A L I F Y         B
  J       I N T E R V A L
  I M P A C T       L     T
  N       T A I L G A T E
  X       K       O     L
          E       W     E
```

```
C H E C K E R E D
  F L A G
```

Sudoku (page 14)

5	2	6	7	4	1	9	8	3
8	1	7	2	9	3	5	6	4
3	4	9	6	5	8	2	1	7
6	9	1	3	8	5	4	7	2
2	8	4	9	1	7	3	5	6
7	5	3	4	2	6	1	9	8
4	3	8	5	7	9	6	2	1
1	6	5	8	3	2	7	4	9
9	7	2	1	6	4	8	3	5

Hashi (page 14)

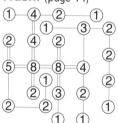

Elevator Words (page 15)

1. CAR pool; 2. pool party; 3. party line;
4. line dance; 5. dance floor; 6. floor
board; 7. board GAME

Alley Shots (pages 16–17)

```
B E N Z   S M U G   T W A
R A C E   T O R O   R A G
A R A B   I T S N O U S E
S P A R E C H A N G E
      A R K   A L G O L
A I M   I M A M   E R G O
S T R I K E P A Y D I R T
T E R N   N O T E   T E S
A M O C O       T A G
    G U T T E R S N I P E
O V E R T A K E   O K A Y
B A R   E X E S   M E R E
I N S   R I D S   E A T S
```

Cross Count (page 18)

²t	⁸h	¹a	²t	13
⁵e	¹a	⁵s	⁵e	12
¹a	²r	²k	¹s	13
³l	⁵e	²s	²t	11
11	23	5	10	

Cluster (page 19)

16　19　17
16　35　36　17
51　71　53
122　124
246

Calcu-doku (page 19)

3	4	1	2
2	3	4	1
4	1	2	3
1	2	3	4

Honeycomb Maze (page 20)

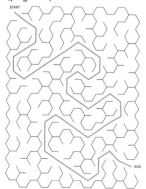

Spell Math! (page 20)

Two + eleven = thirteen

Crazy Circles (page 21)

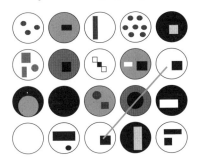

Word Ladder (page 21)

CRAVE, crane, craze, graze, grace, TRACE

Word-a-Maze: Vital Sign (page 22)

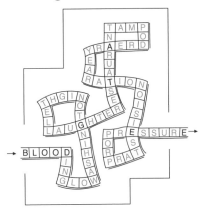

Kakuro (page 23)

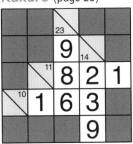

L'adder (page 23)

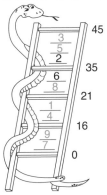

$$\frac{3}{5}$$ 45

2

$$\frac{6}{8}$$ 35

21

$$\frac{1}{4}$$ 16

$$\frac{9}{7}$$ 0

Active Scramblegram (page 24)

EATTHILCS
ATHLETICS

Add-a-Letter (page 25)

1. ear-bear-beard
2. ram-cram-cramp
3. pit-spit-spite
4. art-part-party
5. lop-slop-slope
6. ape-cape-caper
7. men-amen-amend

Answers

Arrow Web (page 26)

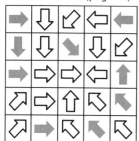

Sudoku (page 26)

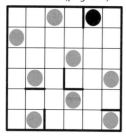

Marbles (page 27)

Weather Word Search
(page 28)

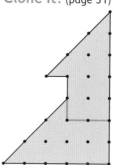

1-2-3 (page 29)

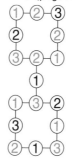

XOXO (page 29)

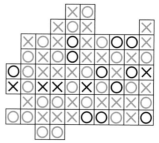

Word Jigsaw (page 30)

Perfect Score (page 30)

$80 + 10 + 10 = 100$

Clone It! (page 31)

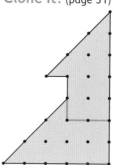

This Is the Day (pages 32–33)

P	O	W	■	T	T	O	P	■	S	M	U	G
O	D	E	■	H	E	R	E	■	P	A	T	E
M	O	R	N	I	N	G	P	R	A	Y	E	R
P	R	E	E	N	S	■	U	P	R	O	S	E
■	■	T	A	I	■	P	M	T	■	■	■	■
B	U	S	■	I	O	N	■	A	P	S	E	■
A	F	T	E	R	N	O	O	N	N	A	P	S
S	O	Y	A	■	■	H	M	O	■	C	A	T
■	■	R	A	N	■	I	T	E	■	■	■	■
I	N	A	T	I	E	■	T	I	T	A	N	S
N	I	G	H	T	W	A	T	C	H	M	A	N
K	L	E	E	■	E	L	E	E	■	A	T	A
S	E	E	N	■	L	A	D	D	■	H	O	P

Kakuro (page 34)

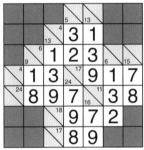

Cross Count (page 34)

²t	⁸h	⁷y	17
⁵w	⁶o	⁵e	16
⁶o	⁷p	²t	15
13	21	14	

Perfect Harmony by Alpha Sleuth™ (page 35)

MUSIC MAKERS

It's a Jungle Out There! (page 36)

Missing Connections (page 37)

Calcu-doku (page 38)

2	5	3	1	4
1	2	4	3	5
5	3	1	4	2
3	4	2	5	1
4	1	5	2	3

Word Columns (page 38)

Now that we have reached the moon and flown beyond the stars, maybe we should take another try at getting pigeons off public buildings.

169

Answers

XOXO (page 39)

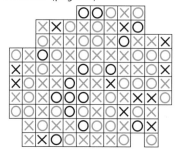

Marbles (page 39)

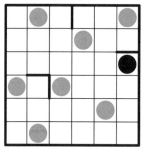

Cast-a-Word (page 40)

1. A F M N S Z
2. B C I P R W
3. D E H J T Y
4. G L O U V X

Cross Count (page 40)

⁶f	¹a	⁹r	⁴m	20
¹a	³l	⁶o	⁵e	15
¹s	⁷p	⁶o	²t	16
²t	⁶o	²t	⁵e	15
10	17	23	16	

Pampered Pups (page 41)

1. groomer's hair turned dark; 2. hearts on uniform; 3. bottle missing; 4. shelves have no sides; 5. clock has different time; 6. picture changed; 7. pocket on uniform missing; 8. bow vanished; 9. bone placed on dog bed; 10. no food in dish; 11. glove added; 12. door gone from cabinet; 13. dog's tongue is out; 14. brush changed position

Rhyme Time (page 42)

1. yule mule; 2. pass mass; 3. lent tent; 4. holy goalie; 5. flock jock; 6. choir liar; 7. cross boss; 8. church birch; 9. bonnet sonnet; 10. bother father

Arrow Web (page 43)

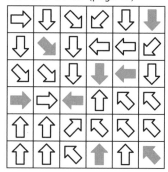

Vex-a-Gon (page 43)

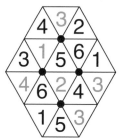

Uncrossed Paths (page 44)

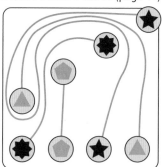

Spelling B (page 45)

```
B E D I Z E N M A N Y
B R U S Q U E R I E E
L B O T R Y O I D A L
E R Y G H A V B E B D
N Y E E A E N S U E A
N O T U L N N G S O E
Y L B L E I P S N O B
Y O B U L W A R K S I
S G P E L G L B I N G
G Y D R A T S U B B H
E E S B U R G O N E T
```

Leftover letters read: Many have been stung by spelling bees.

Perfect Score (page 46)

62 + 23 + 15 = 100

Elevator Words (page 46)

1. POTATO salad; 2. salad green; 3. green olive; 4. olive pit; 5. pit stop; 6. stop short; 7. short STRAW

Star Power (page 47)

Name Calling (page 47)

A mother understands what a child does not say.

Revolutionary Crypto-Quote (page 48)

A lie told often enough becomes the truth.
—V. I. Lenin

A Sequence Addressing Freedom (page 48)

The missing letter is S. The sequence: Four score and seven years ago

You Are Here (page 49)

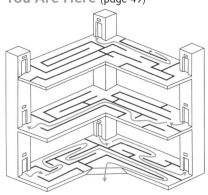

Daffy Definitions (page 50)

```
F E D U P           C   J
    E           G   U   O
    A           L   R   I
    D       G O D S P E E D
    I           C   H   T
    V       T A L L T A L E
    E           U   M   N
    A           B       T
    W                   U
    A                   R
    Y                   E
```

Cube Count (page 51)

There are 16 missing cubes—6 are missing from the top row, 5 are missing from the second row, 4 are missing from the third row, and 1 is missing from the bottom row.

Digital Anagram (page 51)

e-mailed, limeade

Answers

Hashi (page 52)

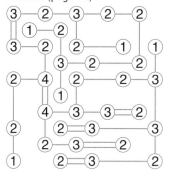

Word Ladder (page 53)

SHAVE, slave, slate, plate, PLATO

Sudoku (page 53)

2	9	8	3	6	7	4	1	5
5	3	1	9	4	8	7	2	6
4	7	6	5	1	2	3	8	9
9	8	5	6	2	4	1	3	7
7	2	3	8	5	1	9	6	4
6	1	4	7	9	3	2	5	8
3	6	7	2	8	9	5	4	1
8	4	2	1	7	5	6	9	3
1	5	9	4	3	6	8	7	2

Kakuro (page 54)

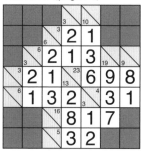

Cluster (page 54)

Auto Showcase by Alpha Sleuth™ (page 55)

STOCKCAR RACING

Word Jigsaw (page 56)

GAG
LARGE
IDIOM
POP

Spell Math! (page 56)

Seven + twelve = ninteteen

Elevator Words (page 57)

1. LIVE wire; 2. wire brush; 3. brush fire;
4. fire alarm; 5. alarm clock; 6. clock face;
7. face LIFT

Presidential Scramblegram
(page 58)

```
  F I L M R O L E
  F I L L M O R E
B V             C G
R A             O O
A N             O D
V B             L O
E U             I L
N R             D I
U E             G L
N N             E E
  H A R R I S O N
  H O R N A I R S
```

```
L L E V C D E A N
C L E V E L A N D
```

L'adder (page 61)

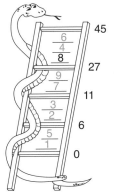

Vex-a-Gon (page 59)

1 4 6
2 3 5 2 1
6 1 4 6 3
   3 5 2

Calcu-doku (page 61)

```
2 4 3 1
1 2 4 3
4 3 1 2
3 1 2 4
```

Cross Count (page 59)

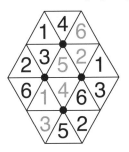

²t	¹a	⁷p	⁵e	15
¹a	⁹b	⁶r	¹a	13
³c	³l	⁶o	²t	14
²t	⁵e	¹s	¹s	9
8	11	23	9	

Dissection (page 60)

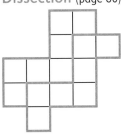

Prince Albert (pages 62–63)

```
U S A G E     P L A N K
S O L O N   R O O K I E
O F A L L   B A T T I N G
C A R D I N A L S   N O S
          S E A L
A E R A T E   Y A H O O S
G L O V E     B U S C H
E M B E D S   C U R A T E
          W A T T
D A D   F I R S T B A S E
A V E R A G E   A E R O S
H O M E R S   L A G O S
S N I D E     S T O N E
```

Answers

XOXO (page 64)

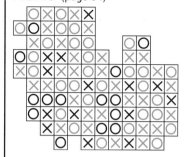

Sudoku (page 64)

8	4	7	2	5	3	6	9	1
3	6	2	7	1	9	4	5	8
5	9	1	8	4	6	2	7	3
4	1	8	3	9	5	7	2	6
7	3	5	6	2	8	1	4	9
6	2	9	1	7	4	8	3	5
2	5	3	4	8	1	9	6	7
9	8	4	5	6	7	3	1	2
1	7	6	9	3	2	5	8	4

Word Columns (page 65)

You know, somebody actually complimented me on my driving today. They left a little note on the windshield; it said "Parking Fine."

Perfect Score (page 65)

44 + 37 + 19 = 100

Missing Connections (page 66)

Word-a-Maze: Big Bang? (page 67)

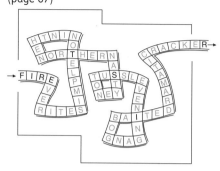

Star Power (page 68)

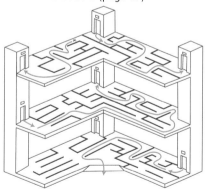

You Are Here (page 69)

Name Calling (page 69)

An elephant is a mouse with an operating system.

Ripe for the Picking by Alpha Sleuth™ (page 70)

GARDEN & GROVE

Marbles (page 71)

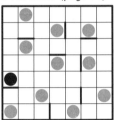

Calcu-doku (page 71)

3	2	1	5	4
1	5	4	2	3
5	4	2	3	1
2	1	3	4	5
4	3	5	1	2

Cast-a-Word (page 72)

1. A B H O T V
2. C I J K U Z
3. D G L M N R
4. E F Q S W Y

Cluster (page 72)

Spell Math! (page 73)

Four + seven = eleven

L'adder (page 73)

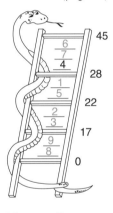

45

$\frac{6}{7}$
$\frac{}{4}$

28

$\frac{1}{5}$

22

$\frac{2}{3}$

17

$\frac{9}{8}$

0

Vex-a-Gon (page 74)

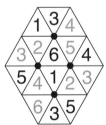

175

Answers

Arrow Web (page 74)

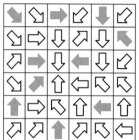

Dissection (page 75)

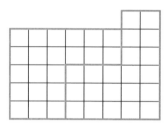

Cross Count (page 75)

²t	⁹r	⁹i	⁷p	**27**
⁹r	⁶o	⁴d	⁵e	**24**
¹a	³l	⁵e	⁵e	**14**
⁷p	³l	¹a	⁵n	**16**
19	**21**	**19**	**22**	

Missing Connections (page 76)

Elevator Words (page 77)

1. TITLE role; 2. role model; 3. model T;
4. T square; 5. square root; 6. root beer;
7. beer PONG

Perfect Score (page 77)

$71 + 17 + 12 = 100$

Change of Scenery by Alpha Sleuth™ (page 78)

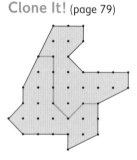

Clone It! (page 79)

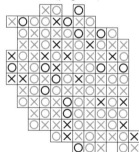

XOXO (page 80)

Code-doku (page 80)

O	G	T	D	L	E	N	A	S
S	N	L	A	G	O	T	E	D
D	E	A	T	N	S	G	O	L
E	A	S	O	T	N	L	D	G
L	T	O	G	A	D	S	N	E
N	D	G	E	S	L	O	T	A
T	L	D	S	O	A	E	G	N
A	O	N	L	E	G	D	S	T
G	S	E	N	T	D	A	L	O

GLADSTONE

Word Columns (page 81)

Astrology rests on a proven principle, namely that if you know the exact positions where the moon and the various planets were when a person was born, you can get this person to give you money.

Once Upon a Time . . .
(pages 82–83)

L	R	N	I	D	D	A	L	A	I	S	R	F	E
I	U	T	M	O	S	L	R	I	G	T	A	O	G
E	M	L	I	O	F	I	I	B	R	U	P	S	L
T	P	H	R	H	E	R	G	O	E	N	U	M	E
O	E	E	G	G	E	H	Y	K	R	N	S	T	T
T	L	S	E	N	C	P	C	W	C	E	Z	W	E
O	S	O	L	I	N	I	T	H	A	K	E	N	R
C	T	O	P	D	I	P	A	O	R	C	L	D	G
E	I	G	P	I	R	D	M	C	C	A	R	F	D
U	L	N	A	R	P	E	E	R	T	R	I	F	N
O	T	E	D	D	G	I	L	I	U	C	L	F	A
I	S	D	A	E	O	P	T	E	N	E	I	D	L
H	K	L	R	R	R	Y	T	D	T	T	A	R	E
C	I	O	L	E	F	E	I	W	E	A	S	A	S
C	N	G	O	L	D	I	L	O	C	K	S	E	N
O	A	I	D	T	H	L	A	L	I	B	A	B	A
N	I	K	S	T	A	C	L	F	A	A	N	E	H
I	S	E	T	I	H	W	W	O	N	S	C	U	H
P	R	I	S	L	T	I	A	N	R	A	N	L	D
E	R	S	E	P	U	C	R	E	T	T	U	B	N

Leftover letters read: Life itself is the most wonderful fairy tale, said Hans Christian Andersen.

Star Power (page 84)

		1	6	7	2	8	
	3	7	4	★	5	★	1
	1	★	2	8	3	4	6
2	8	6	5		7	★	2
4	★	7		2	5	1	8
3	5	1	6	8	★	6	
8	★	2	★	4	3	7	
6	4	7	3	5			

Word Jigsaw (page 84)

V	E	T	
A	M	A	S	S
T	U	L	I	P
	C	R	Y	

Mr. Fix-it (page 85)

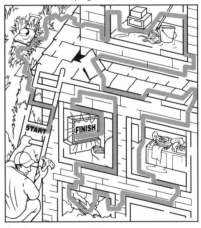

Hot Parade (page 86)

	Name	Surname	Song
1	Amy	Woodlake	River
2	Dustin	Bassett	Sky
3	Saul	Porthome	Waterfall
4	Mark	McArty	Yippee!
5	Girly	Jakeson	Heaven

Number Crossword (page 87)

3	6	1	■
8	7	6	5
5	8	5	8
■	9	6	3

Answers

Calcu-doku (page 87)

3	5	2	1	4
2	4	1	3	5
5	2	3	4	1
4	1	5	2	3
1	3	4	5	2

Uncrossed Paths (page 88)

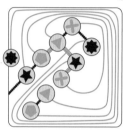

Word-a-Maze: Tiny Dwelling
(page 89)

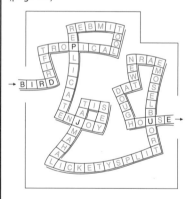

About Face (pages 90–91)

Name Calling (page 92)

Ask about your neighbors,
then buy the house.

Odd-Even Logidoku (page 92)

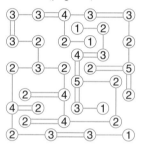

Hashi (page 93)

Cast-a-Word (page 93)

1. A K M S U Y
2. B G H I P X
3. C D E F T V
4. L N O R W Z

Special Days and Holidays
(page 94)

Two more special "days" : Presidents and
Groundhog

178

Manly Scramblegram (page 95)

	N	I	N	E	J	A	M	B	
	B	E	N	J	A	M	I	N	
D	R							L	N
O	A							A	E
N	N							W	W
R	D							R	C
A	O							E	L
L	L							N	A
P	P							C	R
H	H							R	E
	J	O	N	A	T	H	A	N	E
	T	H	A	N	J	O	A	N	

| E | A | I | N | L | A | N | T | H |
| N | A | T | H | A | N | I | E | L |

Perfect Score (page 95)

7 + 28 + 65 = 100

Arrow Web (page 96)

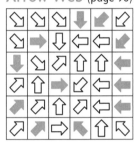

Word Ladder (page 96)

SHELL, shelf, sheaf, shear, sheer,
CHEER

Hamster Treadmill (page 97)

Device B is correct.

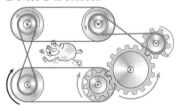

Cube Quandary (page 98)

Cube 5 is impossible.

Cluster (page 98)

Row 1: 25, 5, 10, 15
Row 2: 25, 30, 15, 25, 15
Row 3: 55, 45, 40, 40
Row 4: 100, 85, 80
Row 5: 185, 165
Row 6: 350

Hitori (page 99)

7	2	8	3	7	4	6	2
1	8	6	6	3	2	5	7
7	4	5	7	1	1	1	2
3	7	4	2	1	8	7	2
2	7	4	6	8	3	4	1
6	7	2	4	7	4	1	8
8	3	7	1	7	6	2	5
5	3	3	2	6	7	8	4

Get It Straight (page 100)

Digital Sudoku (page 100)

4	5	2	1	6	3
3	6	1	5	4	2
1	4	5	2	3	6
6	2	3	4	1	5
5	1	6	3	2	4
2	3	4	6	5	1

Answers

Twisted Path (page 101)

Grid Fill (page 101)

A	L	T	E	R	S
S	N	A	P	P	Y
H	A	R	D	L	Y
S	C	H	O	O	L
S	T	R	E	A	K
N	E	E	D	L	E
C	R	E	D	I	T

Cross Count (page 102)

Vex-a-Gon (page 102)

Word Jigsaw (page 103)

		A	D	O
M	A	J	O	R
A	G	A	T	E
P	E	R		

Calcu-doku (page 103)

5	2	1	3	4
4	3	5	2	1
3	4	2	1	5
1	5	3	4	2
2	1	4	5	3

You Are Here (page 104)

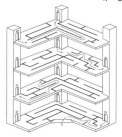

Red, White, Blue, and Green (page 105)

R	G	W	B	B	B	W	R	G
G	W	B	W	R	G	B	R	
B	R	G	R	W	G	B	W	
W	G	B	G	R	B	R	W	
R	W	G	B	B	R	W	G	
B	B	W	G	W	R	G	R	
G	R	R	W	G	B	W	B	
W	B	R	R	G	W	G	B	

1-2-3 (page 106)

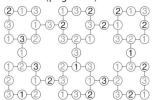

Arrow Web (page 106)

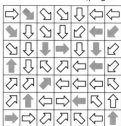

Word-a-Maze: Car Igniter (page 107)

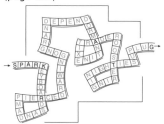

180

XOXO (page 108)

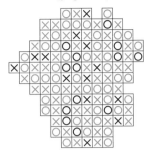

Hashi (page 108)

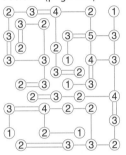

Perfect Score (page 109)

43 + 43 + 14 = 100

Odd-Even Logidoku (page 109)

8	4	7	5	1	9	3	2	6
9	6	3	2	8	4	1	5	7
2	1	5	7	6	3	4	8	9
5	9	4	1	2	8	7	6	3
7	2	1	4	3	6	8	9	5
6	3	8	9	5	7	2	1	4
4	5	2	6	7	1	9	3	8
3	7	6	8	9	2	5	4	1
1	8	9	3	4	5	6	7	2

Uncrossed Paths (page 110)

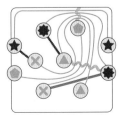

Digital Sudoku (page 111)

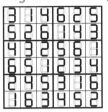

Cluster (page 111)

Get It Straight (page 112)

Cross Count (page 113)

²t	⁹r	⁵e	¹s	17
⁵w	¹a	⁹i	²t	17
¹a	³c	⁹r	⁵e	18
¹s	⁵e	⁵e	⁴m	15
9	18	28	12	

Calcu-doku (page 113)

6	2	1	4	3	5
2	4	5	3	6	1
1	6	2	5	4	3
4	5	3	6	1	2
5	3	6	1	2	4
3	1	4	2	5	6

Answers

Word Jigsaw (page 114)

B	I	G		
O	C	E	A	N
B	E	L	L	E
	S	E	W	

Vex-a-Gon (page 114)

Sudoku (page 115)

2	9	4	3	5	1	6	8	7
8	3	7	6	2	9	1	4	5
1	5	6	8	4	7	3	9	2
7	6	9	4	3	2	8	5	1
3	4	1	5	9	8	7	2	6
5	8	2	1	7	6	9	3	4
6	2	5	7	8	3	4	1	9
9	7	3	2	1	4	5	6	8
4	1	8	9	6	5	2	7	3

Word Ladder (page 115)

DARK, dart, tart, tare, tyre, PYRE

Mondrianize It! (page 116)

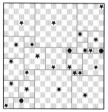

Perfect Score (page 116)

15 + 22 + 63 = 100

Kakuro (page 117)

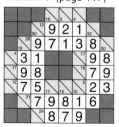

Cube Quandary (page 117)

E is opposite H.
A is opposite X.
N is opposite Y.

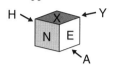

Dance Fever (pages 118–119)

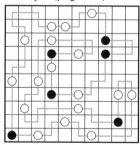

Leftover letters read: ballroom, bolero, hoedown, and stomp are a few more.

Masyu (page 120)

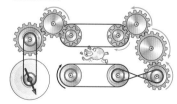

Hamster Treadmill (page 121)

Clockwise

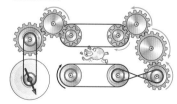

Star Power (page 121)

Digital Sudoku (page 122)

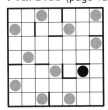

Word Columns (page 122)

An old lady once asked the dispatcher of a local trucking company if they could ship an antique mirror to her sister in Toronto. The dispatcher says, "I don't know madam, I'd have to look into it first."

Cast-a-Word (page 123)

1. A B D G W X
2. C E S T U V
3. F M N O P R
4. H I K L Y Z

Marbles (page 123)

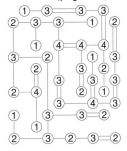

Name Calling (page 124)

Man should live if only to satisfy his curiosity.

Hitori (page 124)

4	6	4	5	3	8	5	2
6	7	1	2	5	2	4	6
6	3	2	5	8	4	1	7
6	4	8	6	4	3	2	3
3	2	4	5	7	1	2	5
2	3	3	7	1	3	5	8
5	1	5	4	6	7	8	3
1	6	6	3	4	5	7	2

The Friendly Skies by Alpha Sleuth™ (page 125)

Elevator Words (page 126)

1. MINUTE book; 2. book club; 3. club steak; 4. steak house; 5. house paint; 6. pain roller; 7. roller BEARING

Hashi (page 127)

Twenty-four Jumble (page 127)

$7 \times 3 - 1 + 4 = 24$ or
$7 \times 3 + 4 - 1 = 24$

Answers

XOXO (page 128)

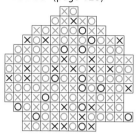

Cross Count (page 128)

The Rumor Mill by Alpha Sleuth™ (page 129)

Fences (page 132)

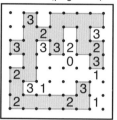

Logidoku (page 132)

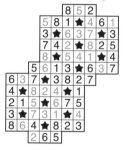

Star Power (page 133)

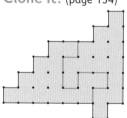

Clone It! (page 134)

The Crossword Without a Theme (pages 130–131)

A	J	A	R		R	O	E		H	A	R	P
V	I	T	A	M	I	N	D		O	V	E	R
O	N	T	H	E	P	L	U	S	S	I	D	E
W	X	Y		G	U	Y		A	E	S	O	P
			Z	A	P		E	M	S			
J	A	P	E			C	A	B		A	H	A
F	R	E	N	C	H	Q	U	A	R	T	E	R
K	E	G		Z	E	D		N	E	W	T	
			V	E	X		V	W	S			
A	Z	T	E	C		D	O	E		L	O	S
W	E	I	G	H	E	D	I	N	W	I	T	H
E	T	N	A		B	A	C	T	E	R	I	A
S	A	Y	S		B	Y	E		B	A	S	H

Calcu-doku (page 135)

5	3	2	4	6	1
2	6	5	1	4	3
4	1	6	3	2	5
1	5	4	2	3	6
6	4	3	5	1	2
3	2	1	6	5	4

Word Columns (page 135)

"Thinking good thoughts is not enough. Doing good deeds is not enough. Seeing others follow your good examples is enough."

Vex-a-Gon (page 136)

Identity Parade (page 136)

The Straight & Narrow by Alpha Sleuth™ (page 137)

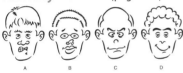

Swarm of S's (page 138)

1. sails; 2. salami (or sausage); 3. sandwich;
4. sash (window); 5. saucer; 6. shadows;
7. shell; 8. ship; 9. shoes (or sneakers);
10. sill; 11. sink; 12. slacks; 13. smile;
14. soap; 15. stool; 16. strings; 17. sun;
18. sweater; 19. sword

Logidoku (page 138)

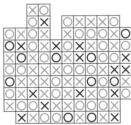

Word Ladder (page 139)

Answers may vary.
TINY, tins, tons, togs, tugs, hugs, HUGE

Perfect Score (page 139)

$33 + 33 + 34 = 100$

Red, White, Blue, and Green (page 140)

G	R	B	R	B	W	W	G
B	W	G	W	G	R	B	R
W	B	B	G	G	R	W	R
G	R	W	R	W	B	G	B
R	G	R	W	B	W	B	G
B	W	G	B	R	G	R	W
W	B	W	G	R	G	R	B
R	G	R	B	W	B	G	W

XOXO (page 141)

Spell Math! (page 141)

Eight + twelve = twenty

185

Answers

The Whole Shebang
(pages 142–143)

Get It Straight (page 144)

1-2-3 (page 145)

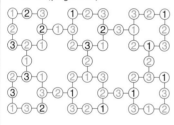

Sudoku (page 145)

9	1	8	3	7	2	5	6	4
6	2	4	5	1	9	3	7	8
3	7	5	4	8	6	2	1	9
5	6	2	1	4	3	8	9	7
1	3	7	6	9	8	4	5	2
4	8	9	7	2	5	6	3	1
8	9	6	2	5	7	1	4	3
2	4	3	9	6	1	7	8	5
7	5	1	8	3	4	9	2	6

Kakuro (page 146)

Marbles (page 146)

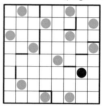

Gridiron Prizes (page 147)

	Name	Surname	Position	Team
1	Chris	Jogger	Quarterback	Irklands
2	Dogger	Lump	Running back	Toxins
3	Forrester	Idle	Wingback	Beckonheres
4	Baz	Keen	Fullback	Stoolers
5	Eddie	Gazelle	Slotback	48ers
6	Abel	Hitman	Center	Wishingtan

Star Power (page 148)

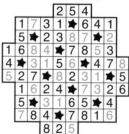

Word Columns (page 148)

Have you ever noticed how a concert audience will applaud a familiar encore after a few bars have been played? They are not applauding the performer or the music. They are applauding themselves because they recognized it.

Word-a-Maze: Choppers
(page 149)

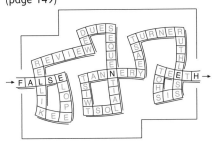

Clone It! (page 150)

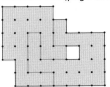

Calcu-doku (page 151)

2	5	3	4	6	1
5	3	2	1	4	6
4	1	6	5	2	3
1	6	5	2	3	4
3	2	4	6	1	5
6	4	1	3	5	2

Digital Sudoku (page 151)

Vex-a-Gon (page 152)

XOXO (page 152)

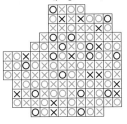

We'll Be A-MAZEd (page 153)

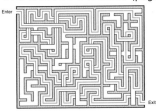

City Down Under (page 153)

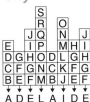

Hashi (page 154)

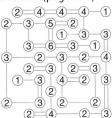

Answers

Cross Count (page 154)

i	m	p	s	21
c	o	a	l	13
e	r	i	e	28
r	e	n	d	23
26	24	22	13	

(with small clue numbers: i⁹, m⁴, p⁷, s¹; c³, o⁶, a¹, l³; e⁵, r⁹, i⁹, e⁵; r⁹, e⁵, n⁹, d⁴)

Logidoku (page 155)

1	3	7	4	9	8	5	6	2
8	2	5	6	7	1	4	9	3
6	4	9	2	3	5	1	7	8
3	6	5	1	3	2	9	2	4
4	5	2	7	6	9	3	8	6
3	9	1	8	2	4	7	5	6
2	6	4	3	5	7	8	1	9
9	7	8	5	4	2	6	3	5
5	1	3	9	8	6	2	4	7

Fences (page 156)

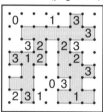

Word Jigsaw (page 156)

```
    M U M
O P E R A
I R O N Y
L O W
```

Uncrossed Paths (page 157)

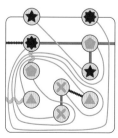

Identity Parade (page 157)

A   B   C   D

This One Will Floor You
(pages 158–159)

```
EKED ANNALS OPS
LEGO BOOBOO NRA
KNOCKONWOOD LOS
   SOD HOMONYMS
HAM PELE MYOPE
ESAI SARAH TNTS
SSGTS TELAVIV
ANIMATE STAMINA
 CANASTA TENOR
LACY STACK SYNE
ABABA KEEP LEA
ARRESTEE EEL
GAP CUTTINGARUG
EDE ADHERE ROSY
RET PENNED DEEM
```

Elevator Words (page 160)

1. AMAZING Grace; 2. Grace Kelly;
3. kelly green; 4. Green Peace; 5. peace
treaty; 6. treaty port; 7. port WINE

Calcu-doku (page 161)

3	5	1	4	2	6
6	2	4	1	5	3
5	3	6	2	1	4
1	4	2	6	3	5
2	6	5	3	4	1
4	1	3	5	6	2

Spell Math! (page 161)

Seven + thirteen = twenty

Name Calling (page 162)

It's kind of fun to do the impossible.

Cluster (page 162)

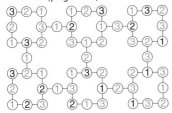

1-2-3 (page 163)

Perfect Score (page 163)

$85 + 13 + 2 = 100$

Symbol Value (page 164)

■ = 20

□ = 12

O = 16

● = 24

Twenty-four Jumble
(page 164)

$3 \times 8 \div 6 \times 5 + 4 = 24$

Index